'*Beyond Grievance* is a hea⎯ to the left to abandon vic⎯ celebrate the varied and ex⎯ ethnic minority groups and ⎯⎯⎯⎯⎯ all of us.'

Katharine Birbalsingh, headteacher of the Michaela School

'When it comes to the intensifying national debates around identity politics, tribalism and social solidarity, Rakib Ehsan's is a compelling voice. Unafraid to ruffle the feathers of self-declared liberals and progressives, he speaks and writes with fluency, passion and – most crucially – a searing honesty. This book deserves the widest attention.'

Paul Embery, author of *Despised: Why the Modern Left Loathes the Working Class*

'Faith, family and flag are hugely important to many black and Asian Britons. Rakib Ehsan's insightful book busts the many myths that the liberal left likes to tell about Britain's diversity and shows that there is strength in the traditional values of our ethnic minority communities.'

Lord Maurice Glasman, author of *Blue Labour*

'Rakib Ehsan is one of the most uninhibited and effective young voices speaking up for the socially conservative left. The fact that he does so as a proud ethnic-minority Briton finding common cause with the country's left-behind, post-industrial communities makes him a challenging figure for both main political parties. On ground prepared by Blue Labour and Red Toryism, Ehsan could be helping to forge an important new coalition. This book is its manifesto.'

David Goodhart, author of *The Road to Somewhere*

'For too long, ethnic-minority Britons have been stereotyped as a poor, downtrodden and marginalised singular group. Rakib Ehsan's refreshing and much-needed book challenges this lazy narrative, instead shedding light on the patriotic, optimistic and hard-working ethos that runs through so many ethnic minority communities.'

Inaya Folarin Iman, founder of the Equiano Project

'Rakib Ehsan takes the Left on a journey, sometimes at turbo-speed. We see a movement which often cohered around the Labour Party really losing its way. The car crash happens as it deserts its own traditional working class for the mad race politics of America. Britain's ethnic minorities hold up a mirror to the soul of the left who have forgotten aspiration, faith, the family, patriotism and the rule of law.'

Lord Tony Sewell, educationalist and former Chair of
the Commission on Race and Ethnic Disparities

'Rakib Ehsan makes a compelling case for the modern British left to reject identitarian politics and refrain from framing every issue around race. Instead, Ehsan importantly argues that more focus should be placed on a social policy that has families at the heart of it. This is a sensible starting point for modern-day Britain.'

Wasiq Wasiq, co-founder of Muslims Against Antisemitism

BEYOND GRIEVANCE

What the Left Gets Wrong
About Ethnic Minorities

RAKIB EHSAN

FORUM

This paperback edition published by Forum 2024
First published in Great Britain by Forum, an imprint of Swift Press 2023

1 3 5 7 9 8 6 4 2

Typesetting and text design by Tetragon, London
Printed and bound in Great Britain by CPI Group (UK) Ltd, Croydon, CR0 4YY

A CIP catalogue record for this book is available from the British Library

ISBN: 9781800751064
eISBN: 9781800751057

CONTENTS

ACKNOWLEDGEMENTS

I owe a debt of gratitude to a number of people who helped me make this book a reality.

My editor at Forum, Dr George Owers, has been a fantastic source of support and encouragement. He deserves great credit for this book's very existence, along with my literary agent Matthew Hamilton and Swift Press publisher Mark Richards. I must also thank my copy-editor Alex Middleton, as well as my typesetter Alex Billington.

I am fortunate to have benefited from the support I have received from editors across a variety of publications over the years. This includes the daring and passionate team at Sp!ked, which has given me the licence to write hard-hitting articles on admittedly sensitive matters of multiculturalism, identity and integration. Having authored multiple pieces for the *Daily Mail* in recent times, I must thank the likes of Oliver Thring and Andrew Yates. I am thankful to former and current comment editors at *The Telegraph*, who have given my thoughts a platform – including Madeline Grant, Sherelle Jacobs,

Olivia Utley, Mutaz Ahmed and Sam Ashworth-Hayes. Both John Ashmore and Alys Denby deserve my thanks for taking on pieces I have authored for CapX over the years. At UnHerd, I must thank James Billot for publishing my digestible posts on social and political attitudes within British ethnic minorities.

There is a string of people whom I admire a great deal – they helped to shape my thinking on matters of society and politics. They include Sir Trevor Phillips, Dr Tony Sewell, Dr Samir Shah, Professor Swaran Singh, David Goodhart and Katharine Birbalsingh. I also appreciate the conversations I have had in recent times with Professor Will Jennings, who has encouraged me to try to become an inclusive liberal–conservative 'bridger' in my field (which is admittedly difficult at times, being as headstrong, stubborn and argumentative as I am!). I must offer my thanks to the two academics who supervised my PhD at Royal Holloway, University of London: Dr James Sloam and Professor Oliver Heath. Another individual who deserves a special mention for reviewing my work in recent times is a young English conservative philosopher who is certainly one to watch out for – Dr Jake Scott.

I have to thank my home town of Luton. I concede that it may not have the greatest reputation, but some of the most patriotic, family-oriented and community-spirited people I know – spanning a variety of races, ethnicities and faiths – are Lutonians. They are salt-of-the-earth folk – decent-hearted traditionalists with a strong sense of fairness and justice. I would also like to thank Britain for providing me with the opportunities and freedoms to live a truly satisfying life. The country has given me so much – I hope that one day I can honestly say to myself that I gave her back my fair share.

Most of all, I must express my gratefulness to my immediate family – especially my angel mother Nasrin. Born and raised in Bangladesh, she is referred to in this book as the greatest British patriot I know. I am honoured to belong to my family, which has provided me with immeasurable amounts of love, support and encouragement. I will do everything in my power to continue making them proud.

INTRODUCTION

Britain is at a crossroads. While I am firmly of the view that it is one of the most successful examples of a multi-racial democracy in the post-Second World War world, we find ourselves in challenging times. While the UK has spent much of the twenty-first century 'nation-building' in faraway lands such as Afghanistan – to no great effect – ours seems to be an increasingly fragmented society with depressingly low levels of political trust. There is a certain ridiculousness involved in spearheading grand 'nation-building' exercises abroad when you're one of the leading countries in the world for family breakdown and loneliness among the elderly – worrying features of the British mainstream that I talk about a fair bit in this book. Left-behind neighbourhoods – economically deprived, socially atomised, culturally demoralised – can be found in every corner of Britain. Believe me, I am more positive and optimistic than most – but the current social, political and economic situation is not sustainable. Britain needs a mature and traditional social-democratic party more than ever – one which emphasises the value of stability and security.

There have been two significant developments in recent times which have had extraordinary impacts on our national socio-political discourse and exposed the lack of intellectual maturity and moral decency on the left: the UK's decision to leave the European Union and the emergence of the Black Lives Matter (BLM) movement. Back in June 2016, the former both revealed and intensified social and political divides. One of the sharpest dividing lines between Leave and Remain voters was their respective perceptions of cultural diversity in modern Britain and the degree to which they were satisfied with the democratic system. Leave voters were more likely to prioritise immigration as a policy concern, hold more negative views on multiculturalism and express dissatisfaction with the way democracy works in Britain. None of these are unreasonable positions to hold, when one considers how the British political classes have been intensely relaxed over the toxic mixture of mass immigration and failed integration outcomes.

Some of the explanations provided for Brexit were beyond woeful. Former Liberal Democrat leader Sir Vince Cable argued that it was driven by 'white nostalgia' – a longing for a bygone era when Britain had a monoracial society.[1] He was not alone – a swathe of pro-Remain politicians, journalists and academics sought to present Brexit as a racist project: a divisive enterprise driven by swivel-eyed provincial reactionary throwbacks who could not cope with the number of brown and black faces in Britain (which, far more often than not, originated from non-EU countries).

Julia Ward, the former Labour MEP for the North West England region, labelled Brexit a 'right wing fascist coup'.[2] When one considers the longstanding tradition of Eurosceptic left politics, embodied by historical Labour Party figures such as Tony Benn and Peter Shore, it is clear that this shameless caricature of Brexit is a fundamental misrepresentation. Then we had the ultra-identitarian MP for Tottenham, David Lammy, who compared the pro-Leave European Research Group (ERG) faction of the Conservative Party to the Nazis and those who were complicit in the enforcement of apartheid in South Africa.[3] I am not sure ERG members such as Steve Baker and Jacob Rees-Mogg quite resemble the likes of Adolf Hitler (or Daniël François Malan, for that matter). For a man of black-Caribbean origin to exploit the atrocities that occurred under Nazism and the racially motivated brutalisation under apartheid in order to score cheap points over Brexit was shameful – as was the sheer lack of condemnation it was met with within the Labour Party.

These simplistic narratives peddled by supposedly enlightened sophisticates are not only grossly offensive but fundamentally detached from the reality on the ground. And, crucially, they 'whitewash' the fact that one in three ethnic-minority voters backed Brexit and decided – for a multitude of reasons – that the UK is better off outside the EU. My home town of Luton – where I have lived for three decades – has a majority-non-white population and delivered a Leave vote of 56.5 per cent.[4] This included patriotic Gujarati Hindu and Punjabi Sikh elders who believed that the UK needed to extricate itself from what they considered the sclerotic and inefficient EU and strengthen its ties with the Commonwealth. These are salt-of-the-earth, community-spirited people who take pride in their British identity – and do not feel an ounce of 'Europeanness'. And neither were they willing to accept a UK immigration regime in which, under EU freedom of movement, predominantly white-European migrants were the beneficiaries of preferential treatment.

Data suggests that Euroscepticism in Britain's South Asian population – particularly the UK's Indian ethnic group – was stronger than was generally thought ahead of the June 2016 referendum on EU membership. Look at Osterley and Spring Grove. A relatively affluent, non-white-majority ward in the west-London borough of Hounslow, it returned a Leave vote of 63.4 per cent.[5] Defying the wider national trend, non-white ethnicity was associated with voting Leave in the two multi-ethnic west-London boroughs of Hounslow and Ealing. Along with Luton, a number of jurisdictions with large South Asian populations also delivered Leave votes: Hillingdon (56.4 per cent), Slough (54.3 per cent) and Bradford (54.2 per cent).[6] All have South Asian populations of 25 per cent or above.[7] It is fair to assume that these figures relied on healthy support for Brexit among voters of South Asian origin.

I have wondered if political journalists and correspondents are aware of these voting patterns. If so, where were the vox pops with pro-Brexit, first-generation South Asian elders in large towns such as Luton and Slough? How many economically secure west Londoners of Indian origin have been asked by mainstream media outlets to articulate their Eurosceptic views? Why did the homeowning, higher-status workers in Osterley, many of whose origins are in Gujarat and the Punjab, not vote in a way – according to liberal convention – that their socio-economic class would predict? Their views could have added great value to the national coverage as to how the Leave vote came about – something that still seems to mystify many. London-based journalists didn't have to visit working-men's clubs in the north or pubs in the provincial Midlands to find Brexit voters – they could have looked no further than the mandirs and gurdwaras of west London.

Osterley is a ten-minute drive from Sky News HQ, and comfortably under an hour from BBC Broadcasting House on the Tube. So why the myopia? Perhaps it is simply a case of the media being incredibly lax, not with their travel plans but with their research. But perhaps it was too much of a challenge to the narrative that the June 2016 Leave result was the product of nostalgic, left-behind, poorly educated, misinformed white working-class folk – low-resourced 'simpletons' driven by their basic jingoistic impulses. This kind of patronising and condescending narrative has tragically gained a foothold in liberal-left politics – that Brexit was brought on by prejudicial and witless white people in the provinces who were simply not knowledgeable or cultured enough to form their own view on the UK's place in the EU.

Media clips of Leave voters were too often restricted to white working-class people in abandoned coastal towns and ailing post-industrial districts left battered by the harsh winds of globalisation. Soundbites such as 'Make Britain great again' and 'Put the "great" back in Great Britain' were typical. As well as featuring on primetime TV, these segments have been pushed out as digestible clips on social media platforms such as Facebook and Twitter. The idea of Brexit as a 'white working-class revolt' – an uprising of the nostalgic in stagnant regions abandoned by the London-centric political establishment – has some truth in it. But what is also true is that mainstream coverage of 'Brexit Britain' illustrated why the media cannot be fully trusted to delve into why important political and social events, such as the Leave vote in June 2016, take place. The appetite for thorough investigation and the reporting of realities has increasingly given way to the ideologically motivated peddling of reductive narratives.

In the case of Brexit, the dominant media narratives failed spectacularly to capture the complex nature of British Euroscepticism. Brexit exposed an unfortunate reality: that the media's commitment to reporting the facts, pure and simple, leaves a lot to be desired. And while this could be the product of bad journalism and poor research, there is also the possibility that the media's 'research and inform' function has been usurped by a role as 'narrative manufacturer'. The reality is that Brexit was a thoroughly multi-ethnic, cross-class enterprise – one could even say a socio-political corrective, unified by a desire to free the UK from a dogmatic and unstable EU political project, restore national sovereignty over important policy issues such as immigration and revitalise a democratic system that was being hollowed out in the name of distant technocratic managerialism. If Brexit is not treated as a catalyst for social, economic and democratic renewal, that is ultimately a failure of our ruling political classes – dominated by self-serving incompetents obsessed with vanity projects.

Brexit, which both highlighted and exacerbated cultural fault lines in British society, was followed by another seismic socio-political development: the emergence of the American-established BLM movement in the UK. Following the police murder of African American George Floyd in the US state of Minnesota on 25 May 2020, a wave of BLM demonstrations took place in the United States – from California on the west coast to New York on the east coast. But the impact of Floyd's death was not confined to the United States, with protests taking place across the Anglosphere and much of the West. A case of police brutality in Minneapolis sparked nationwide protests in Britain. As well as being held in major cities such as London, Birmingham, Manchester, Liverpool, Leeds, Bristol and Newcastle, the BLM protests have reached as far as the Isle of Wight off the English south coast and the Shetland Islands in Scotland.

In my view, it is hugely regrettable that events in the United States have had such a notable impact on contemporary British civil discourse. Some have argued that the wave of BLM demonstrations collectively represented a seismic social shift which has drawn attention to problems of 'systemic racism' and 'police brutality' in the UK. Indeed, it has been suggested that Britain has 'failed to deal with systemic racism' and that while racism in the UK 'may attract less global attention than in the United States… it is no less present'.[8] Some commentators have gone so far as to suggest that 'systemic racism exists in the UK at every level of government and society', while the impact of the Covid-19 pandemic on Britain's ethnic minorities has been framed by mayor of London Sadiq Khan as an 'injustice'.[9] In a video included in a tweet containing the hashtag #BlackLivesMatter, former shadow home secretary Diane Abbott referred to the Covid-19 outcomes for black, Asian and minority ethnic (BAME) communities as 'a form of violence'.[10] As I explain in Chapter 1, the left-wing identitarian discourse surrounding Covid-19 outcomes has been woefully simplistic.

Demonstrating the degree to which American cultural politics has been imported into the UK by the contemporary British left, BLM protestors have cried 'Don't shoot' at British police officers – despite the overwhelming majority being unarmed on everyday duty (a policing model that commands widespread support within the profession itself). Labour MP Dawn Butler, who represents the London constituency of Brent Central and no stranger to inflammatory language, called for the government to get its 'knee off the neck of the Black, African Caribbean, Asian and minority ethnic community' in a House of Commons statement.[11] This was not simply the importation of US racial politics, but the crude weaponisation of a police murder in Minnesota by an elected parliamentarian who was speaking at the heart of British democracy. Such aggressive imitation of racial-grievance politics from the United States has undermined the credibility of the British left – with an uncompromising identitarian tribalism taking hold in Labour's parliamentary party and key decision-making bodies. The exploitation of race by Labour figures such as public-policy 'analyst' Anneliese Dodds means the left is failing to make enlightening contributions to the British marketplace of policy ideas.

Labour's embrace of the BLM movement – encapsulated by the cringeworthy photo of leader Sir Keir Starmer and deputy leader Angela Rayner taking the knee – has not necessarily paid dividends. An Opinium poll conducted in November 2020 found that the majority of Brits – 55 per cent – believed that the BLM movement had heightened racial tensions in the UK. This included a plurality of ethnic-minority Britons.[12] Fresher data from YouGov suggests that the British public have become more negative about the direction of race relations since the wave of BLM protests which took place in Britain.

Whereas one in five people (19 per cent) felt that prior to the protests race relations were deteriorating, that figure has increased to 36 per cent for the period since. Only 8 per cent of the general population thinks race relations have improved since the BLM protests.[13]

These figures are troubling, but they are not a great surprise. Moreover, the BLM movement has played its part in the intensification of intra-black animosity in Britain. Black Britons who refuse to toe the BLM line have been labelled by identitarian fanatics as 'coons' and 'Uncle Toms', and accused of being 'race traitors' and 'house Negroes'. This has certainly been the experience of politicians such as Conservative MP and equalities minister Kemi Badenoch and government policy advisor Mercy Muroki, as well as respected race-relations experts such as Sir Trevor Phillips and Dr Tony Sewell. Polling by ICM Unlimited in early 2021 found that 8 per cent of black Britons had faced racial discrimination at the hands of another black person in the past 12 months.[14] Indeed, one in six Brits of black-Caribbean origin has an unfavourable view of co-racial compatriots of African origin.[15] The 'black community' is fast revealing itself to be a fictitious construct that masks serious ethnic and political tensions – and it is further exposed as a mockery when one considers the destructive impact of gang-related violence in London (something which is not talked about all that much by supporters of BLM).

Radical positions associated with or promoted by BLM – such as abolishing police forces, overthrowing the market economy and supporting forms of direct action – are far from popular with black Britons. They go well beyond conventional anti-racist activity and undermine the broader racial-equality cause. The results of ICM Unlimited's polling strongly suggest that the core objectives and political methods of the UK BLM organisation (and the broader BLM social movement) are far from being inclusive and well supported. While avid supporters of the broader movement have portrayed the UK as a fundamentally racist society which has a police-brutality problem, these views are not mainstream and are held by only a minority of people in the general population: only one in ten people in the UK general population supports reduced investment in their own local police force – something that is also a minority view in black-British communities (held by fewer than one in five people).[16] The aggressively anti-capitalist tendencies of BLM are clearly not shared by much of the British public, with only one in four black-British people supporting the replacement of the market economy with a socialist system.[17] With a number of the BLM demonstrations last summer descending into various forms of public disorder, the vast majority of the UK general population – including black Britons – categorically reject the view that tearing down statues, burning the Union flag and damaging business property are acceptable forms of political protest.[18]

Far too many in the Labour Party have supported the core assertions of the broader BLM social movement:

that Britain is a fundamentally racist society blighted by widespread forms of 'systemic racism' and 'structural discrimination'. This is a grossly unfair caricature that is not rooted in reality. This is not to say that there is no room for improvement, for fostering more socially representative and culturally responsive institutions: there is certainly a discussion to be had on strengthening forms of institutional trust. There is also much that can be done in Britain to improve equality of opportunity, bolster police–community relations and enhance the responsiveness of healthcare institutions to the needs of an ever-diversifying population. But most of Britain is tolerant, pro-equality of opportunity and anti-discriminatory in its views. Britain's democratic system of governance – from a general ethnic-minority viewpoint – is perceived to be in generally good shape.

Britain, like all countries, is flawed and imperfect – but this does not change the reality that it remains one of the most successful examples in the world of a democracy which is both multiracial and religiously diverse. With the possible exception of Canada – which traditionally boasts especially high levels of social solidarity and political trust, as well as a strong sense of collective national belonging[19] – Britain is arguably the leading race-relations model for white-majority, multi-ethnic societies. (It is worth noting that Canada has certain advantages: a much smaller population within a far larger land mass, along with a rather open but rigorously selective immigration system. This can be best understood as a liberal–conservative compromise.) Indeed, this was the conclusion drawn by the Parekh report, whose publication in 2000 by the racial-equality think tank the Runnymede Trust was a defining moment in the national discourse surrounding community cohesion in Britain.[20] The leading author, the highly respected Professor Bhikhu Parekh, at the time confidently proclaimed that Britain had some of the best race relations in Europe, arguing that the idea that racism was widespread in British society was a 'partisan and skewed' view. Parekh, who chaired the 23-strong commission set up by the Runnymede Trust, concluded that Britain had a 'much more relaxed' society than other multiracial democracies, such as France, Germany or the United States.[21]

Much of this rings true today. Britain has established itself as a European leader on matters of social cohesion and economic fairness – especially over matters of race. It comfortably outperforms white-majority, multi-ethnic European countries such as France, Germany and the Netherlands when it comes to the provision of anti-discrimination protections on the grounds of race, ethnicity and religion.[22] When it comes to harassment, intimidation and violence towards black people of African descent, the UK fares much better than a host of EU member states – and certainly than the nearby Republic of Ireland.[23] The 2020 Migrant Integration Policy Index (MIPEX) reached the view that people who do suffer from discrimination in the UK can rely on some of the strongest equality bodies in the world.

Overwhelmingly tolerant attitudes towards a range of ethno-religious minorities demonstrate the open-mindedness of the mainstream, as does the general acceptance of interracial relationships which has led to the 'mixed-race' category being the fastest-growing racial group for the last few decades. According to a 2019 study by the think tank British Future, nine in ten people in England reject the view that racial identity is integral to 'Englishness' – with a comfortable majority inclusively framing English identity in terms of civic duty and social contribution.[24] In 'Little England' – supposedly a land of nostalgic, swivel-eyed reactionaries – the majority are far more likely to perceive national identity in terms of what one brings to the table as a citizen than to see it as a question of skin colour and ancestral origins. Inclusive communitarian values – positively contributing towards the well-being of the community, respecting legal obligations and paying taxes towards public services and national security – lie at the heart of mainstream contemporary framings of English identity.

Today it appears that the Runnymede Trust views race relations in the country rather differently. Its summer 2021 report, submitted to the UN's Committee on the Elimination of Racial Discrimination (CERD), concluded that Britain has failed to meet the obligations determined by the International Convention on the Elimination of All Forms of Racial Discrimination (ICERD), that the country is 'deliberately rigged against ethnic minorities' and that 'racism is systemic in England

and impacts the enjoyment of rights of BME groups'.[25] But can the Runnymede Trust be trusted as a professional, level-headed contributor to the race-relations debate? Based on its own output, the organisation essentially argued that, over the last 20 years, Britain has descended from being an internationally reputable model for race relations to a systemically racist society where various spheres of life are deliberately rigged against its own non-white citizens. This is a scorching-hot take – and I suspect it is one that many wouldn't embrace.

Neither will many support the view that the UK government – which has its fair share of flaws – is pursuing a divisive 'white-nationalist' agenda at the expense of British ethnic minorities. Yet this is exactly what the trust's current CEO, Dr Halima Begum, argued in an interview with *The Guardian*.[26] Having personally authored reports on far-right ideologies, I am not sure that a genuinely white-nationalist regime in the Western world would have placed a Gujarati-origin woman, Priti Patel, at the heart of government – one who personally created a bespoke immigration route for Hongkongers and Afghans. In recent times, inward migration from India, Pakistan and Nigeria has risen exponentially under the Conservatives. The Tories – while a largely incompetent and self-serving political institution beholden to corporate interests and boomer wealth – are a centre-right parliamentary party which is generally comfortable with the demographic and cultural diversity that characterises its own country. The only other centre-right party in the Western world that ranks as highly on this front is perhaps the Conservative Party of Canada.

A once-respectable anti-racist organisation, the Runnymede Trust has ceased to be a mature and inclusive voice in Britain's race-relations conversation. But why? Because it is now at the heart of Britain's grievance-industrial complex – a social infrastructure where the financial health of bad-faith actors ultimately rests on the peddling of fundamentally warped interpretations of British society and its institutions. Offering the view that family structures, community dynamics, socio-cultural norms, geographical inequalities and migratory backgrounds can all feed into ethnic and racial disparities is not of any interest to these 'racial-equality' organisations; rather, their preservation and relevance depend on maintaining the 'disparities = discrimination' paradigm. There is a growing band of politically correct television personalities, attention-seeking celebrity entertainers, crank pseudo-intellectual academics, public-sector 'diversity professionals' and race-baiting journalists who are integrating themselves into this moralising and profiteering infrastructure.

The UK's withdrawal from the EU and the emergence of the BLM movement on British shores have contributed to the intensification of racial-grievance politics and the growing vilification of British society and public institutions. With Brexit being grossly caricatured by a disenchanted tribe of anti-Leave progressive activists as a signifier of racial nostalgia in the white-British mainstream, non-white voters who voted against remaining in a bitter, sclerotic and inefficient bloc have been vilified as 'Uncle Toms' and 'executioners of white supremacy'. Black Brits and British Asians who refuse to toe the modern left's identitarian line (that existing racial disparities are direct outputs of institutional discrimination and systemic racism) and believe that the BLM movement has undermined social cohesion in their country have been accused of being 'tokens', 'coconuts' and 'race traitors'. This normalisation of left-wing racism – and it is racism, as it judges individuals by their race – is a growing illness in our democratic society. It also drags British leftist traditions rooted in social solidarity and anti-discrimination through the mud.

Which brings us to the question the book seeks to answer: what is the current state of the modern left's relationship with British ethnic minorities? After decades of providing the Labour Party with comprehensive electoral support (largely the legacy of race-relations legislation passed in the 1970s and the party's traditional ownership of equality issues), are these bonds showing signs of fraying? Is the contemporary British left's unrelenting obsession with racial identity as the primary vector of disadvantage serving to solidify support in British non-white communities, or is it being seen as an unappealing form of paternalistic identitarianism? Is placing matters of race at the forefront of discussions on complex forms of socio-economic disadvantage shoring up the support of family-oriented ethnic-minority people of faith who value personal responsibility and individual initiative, or is it alienating them? Indeed, is the radical cultural liberalism which has come to dominate the mainstream British left even respectful of the more socially conservative values which run deep in ethnic-minority communities?

I fear the answer to the last of these questions is no. As I write this introduction, I see a contemporary British left which could do much more in presenting itself as a credible and relevant government-in-waiting to a largely incompetent and arguably even crooked Conservative Party which has now been in power for well over a decade. As an old-school leftist who blends a strong sense of social justice with a fulfilling, family-oriented tradition-alism, I – like many former Labour voters in Britain – think that the modern left is threatening to turn a once-great party into an amateurish pressure group that is in thrall to a divisive and unpopular identity politics. This is not the promotion of an anti-racist, inclusive politics – rather, the racial and religious 'authenticity' of ethnic-minority people is questioned if they refuse to accept the identitarian agenda. This, alongside the normalisation of anti-democratic sentiments on the left, threatens to hurt Labour's electoral prospects. This is not a wholesome and relatable politics that will win at the ballot box – or one that can help to improve social cohesion and community relations in modern Britain.

While some modern leftists already view me as an 'Uncle Tom', 'House Muslim', 'coconut', 'race traitor' and 'bootlicker' (my personal favourite being 'the Tandoori

Mosley'), I am more than happy to engage with the more sensible and serious elements of the contemporary British left. But part of this process is acknowledging some hard truths. Unless the left recognises that, for all its flaws, Britain remains one of the more successful examples of a post-Second World War multiracial democracy, then it will continue to fail at the ballot box. It will also struggle in an electoral sense if it refuses to challenge forms of political correctness and identity politics which have taken hold in public institutions such as the NHS, schools and the police.

While there is no doubt that the modern Tory Party has its fair share of social liberals and thought-policing marshals, it is the British political left which is defined by politically correct tendencies and divisive identity politics. And that (along with its disastrous second-referendum policy) is largely why the Labour Party has lost many voters in predominantly white, working-class communities, and is now at risk of leaking more votes in ethnic-minority communities which are proud of their national identity, believe that a stable family unit is the finest of social safety nets and hold conservative views on matters of law and order.

It does not fill me with pleasure to see a radical band of hard-left activists and out-of-touch social liberals drag the traditions of the Labour Party into the gutter. Labour's disastrous showing in December 2019 – its worst general-election performance (in terms of seats) since 1935 – was a bitter experience. Living in a predominantly working-class town where trade unionism runs deep in our local communities, I want to see a relatable and competitive Labour Party in British politics. I want to see the contemporary British left bring life-changing, pro-worker initiatives to the table, deliver practical proposals to improve equality of opportunity in the labour market, promote the family and community as critical sources of belonging and rootedness, appreciate people's understandable desire for stability and security, and cultivate inclusive forms of multiethnic patriotism – but, as it stands, it is failing miserably, with our politics being all the poorer for it.

I consider my book part of an intellectual–cultural backlash to much of what has been said on admittedly sensitive matters of race and identity in the UK and the wider Western world. I have no intention to make white people feel guilty over their racial 'fragility' – whether the modern 'anti-racist' likes it or not, you cannot make race-relations progress without the support of decent-hearted and fair-minded whites (who vastly outnumber the racist bigots who are all too often presented by the liberal left as representative of the mainstream). Alienating them by coercing them into a condition of guilt over colonialism is perhaps not the wisest way to go about building a more inclusive multiracial society for the future. American-inspired 'intersectional' theory – obsessed with portraying white males as a hyper-privileged section of society – is of limited value when the one group of pupils who are underperforming in English schools are white working-class boys (often from dysfunctional family backgrounds and run-down communities). The fixation on protected characteristics such as race and gender, in this context, only serves to demonstrate the liberal-left estrangement from the concept of class.

Set against the doom-and-gloom identitarianism which defines much of the modern British left, this book offers a corrective on the current socio-political and socio-economic state of affairs in Britain's ethnic minorities. The actual picture is more positive than many modern progressive activists suggest. There are ethnic-minority groups – all too often overlooked by 'white-privilege' narratives – that now outperform the white-British mainstream in terms of school attainment and labour-market integration. When their existence is acknowledged, they are at times – quite perniciously – branded as 'white-adjacent'. Britain's ethnic minorities are not a marginalised and disempowered collective by any stretch of the imagination. Often belonging to robust family units and tight-knit communities, they are largely appreciative of the anti-discrimination protections and religious freedoms afforded under our democracy.

The moment *Beyond Grievance* was announced, I received an astonishing amount of support and encouragement, mainly from patriotic and communitarian working-class Brits of migrant stock, who thanked me for deciding to invest my time and energy in providing an uplifting challenge to the racial-grievance narratives that now dominate modern-left discourse. These are well and truly the salt of the earth – hard-working, resilient and self-disciplined people of faith who unapologetically defend their 'Family First' philosophy. Having little time for materialistic individualism and divisive identity politics, their lives are defined by the traditional triad of family, faith and flag. Many are former Labour voters – abandoned by a party that once respected their strong sense of fairness and quietly traditional values. I hope, with this first book of mine, I have done them proud.

1

WHY THE LEFT SHOULD DROP 'WHITE PRIVILEGE' THEORIES

Like many other nations, the United States experienced its fair share of struggles during the Covid-19 pandemic. Americans of all racial and ethnic backgrounds have suffered – losing their loved ones, their jobs and their livelihoods. While a swathe of large corporations had a field day as their profits skyrocketed, many of America's small-to-medium-sized businesses – the lifeblood of local communities – have struggled to keep afloat. Men and women of all walks of life, many of whom started their dream enterprises from scratch, are under untold amounts of stress.

Shared anxieties call for messages of social solidarity. However, as president-elect, Joe Biden struck a dreadfully unhelpful tone on this front. On 10 January 2021, the official White House account tweeted: 'Our priority will be Black, Latino, Asian, and Native American owned small businesses, women-owned businesses, and finally having equal access to resources needed to reopen and rebuild.'[1] This was far from a unifying message. It represents the takeover of intersectionality – a framework in which being a white male is viewed as a position of hyper-advantage. 'We will provide comprehensive support to America's small businesses, owned by men and women of different backgrounds who are the backbone of our treasured nation' would have made for a presidential statement of national unity. We should spare a thought for the white, male business owners feeling the pinch in the industrial Midwest – some of whom helped Biden carry states such as Pennsylvania, Michigan and Wisconsin.

Similarly, just before the last US presidential election, vice president Kamala Harris tweeted a video making the case for 'equity' over 'equality'.[2] It finishes with the line: 'Equitable treatment means we all end up at the same place.' In essence, this is a rejection of equality of *opportunity* in favour of equality of *outcome*. The enforcement of this by the federal government is not something much of moderate America will tolerate. Sacrificing equality of opportunity on the altar of 'racial equity' will only stretch the nation's social fabric further – inevitably creating the kind of resentment we saw in those traditionally Democratic, blue-collar counties that became Donald Trump territory. A wholesome progressive politics that blends racial-equality causes with an honest, family-friendly traditionalism could have formed the basis of a new era of Democratic Party dominance; instead, however, the aggressive proliferation of white-privilege theories and the politics of intersectionality have presented fertile ground for a post-Trump Republican recovery.

If recent events have taught us anything, it is that US politics is volatile – things can change very quickly indeed. This was demonstrated by the November 2021 gubernatorial election in the Commonwealth of Virginia, which proved to be a breakthrough moment for the Grand Old Party. In the presidential election held just a year earlier, Biden carried the state with a ten-point advantage over former president Donald Trump. This made the gubernatorial vote a major electoral test for the Democrats under Biden's presidency – one which they were at one point expected to pass with flying colours. In truth, however, it was nothing but a categorical failure. Republican Glenn Youngkin – now governor – secured a stunning victory over Democrat Terry McAuliffe in a state that former Democratic governor Ralph Northam won with ease in 2017. The warning signs were evident throughout the election – if only the Democrats had been capable of some honest introspection.

Youngkin, a successful, Harvard-educated businessman born in the state capital of Richmond, focused on bread-and-butter educational and economic issues as part of a broader family-oriented message, and, alongside Suzanne, his wife of over 25 years, and their four children, was able credibly to promote a quietly traditional brand of conservative politics. These political selling points were effective in the pre-Trump era, and they still are today.

With the United States currently witnessing the proliferation of Critical Race Theory (CRT) and associated
concepts such as 'white privilege' through its school
systems, Youngkin expressed his support for parental
concerns over the divisive nature of such materials being
used in the classroom. In addition to stressing the need
to 'press forward with a curriculum that includes listening
to parents' input', Youngkin spoke of his intention to
'restore excellence in our schools'.[3] Such a message may
seem simplistic, but in a world in which Democrats
are obsessed with radical theories that have trickled
down from the universities, it hit home and helped to
win over moderate independent voters in the suburbs.
Many of these people may not have been keen on seeing
Trump re-elected as president, but they are certainly
not supportive of 'race-conscious education' dominating
school agendas. Overindulging in racial identity politics
and cultural liberalism could facilitate a Republican
comeback. A 2024 GOP presidential candidate who
carries forward the core tenets of Trumpism – economic
populism and cultural conservatism – while also pro-
jecting an image of competence and stability will have
a fighting chance of winning. Perhaps current Florida
governor Ron DeSantis could be the man to lead the
charge?

At this moment, you may well be wondering: 'Why on
earth is Rakib bleating on about the United States in a
book about the British left and the UK's ethnic minorities?' Here's why. In the UK, there is a real danger that the

left will be further seduced by American race politics. The aggressive importation of US-origin pseudo-academic theories – which tend to place racial identity at the heart of understanding very complex forms of social disadvantage and material deprivation – threatens to undermine the respectability of the British anti-racism movement. The 'disparities = discrimination' paradigm is a crudely reductive framework for understanding racial and ethnic differences in areas such as education and employment. The excesses of American left-wing political activism are responsible for framing 'disadvantage' and 'privilege' through the simplistic prism of race, vilifying traditional institutions such as the family and marriage, and aggressively promoting ultra-liberal forms of gender self-identification that pose a fundamental threat to women's rights. Indeed, I would argue that the United States' cultural exportation of radical identity politics is a gift for hostile, anti-Western states that welcome intensifying forms of social fragmentation and moral decay in the Western world. This is ultimately a form of ideological neo-imperialism that is designed to 'civilise' industrialised nations where quietly traditional values – a belief in family, a sense of personal responsibility, scepticism towards gender self-identification – continue to be somewhat influential in mainstream society. It is a cultural poison that threatens to undermine the very foundations of Western civilisation – and represents a fundamental assault on much of what is held dear by traditional ethnic-minority voters in Britain.

Labour's enthusiastic embrace of tribal identity politics and radical social liberalism presented the Conservative Party with an opportunity to build a cross-class, multi-ethnic coalition of voters who are patriotic and aspirational, and have little time for niche minority interests which threaten social solidarity. As it happens, however, the modern Conservative Party has shown very few signs of trying to do so. This shouldn't lead us, however, to give the left a free pass because Labour might win the next election anyway due to the failures of the uninspiring Tories. The modern British left's importation of 'progressive' identitarian initiatives from across the pond does not serve our society well in terms of social cohesion. And nor is it clever politics, in a country where the majority of ethnic-minority citizens expect fairness – not favours – and value their British identity. Pandering to a radical but vocal minority will never help unify diverse societies – it only places them on the dreaded path towards greater social division and cultural fragmentation.

The left-wing identitarian trend we are witnessing in the UK, somewhat influenced by American socio-political discourse surrounding matters of race, is serving to undermine the legacy of the old-fashioned anti-racist politics promoted by a historical figure I admire a great deal: Martin Luther King, Jr. This traditional anti-racism was rooted in the fair allocation of political, legal and social rights and a rational approach to anti-discrimination policy. At the heart of this was the principle of equality of opportunity. This is reflected in MLK's address to the

American Federation of Labor and Congress of Industrial Organizations (AFL–CIO) in December 1961, in which he spoke about 'a dream of equality of opportunity, of privilege and property widely distributed; a dream of a land where men will not take necessities from the many to give luxuries to the few'.[4] At the core of MLK's vision of a post-racial American nation state was the combatting of rampant socio-economic inequalities in access to opportunities, high-quality public services and private ownership.

MLK's anti-racist, social-democratic politics did not only appreciate the human desire to be treated fairly, irrespective of racial background, but also understood that the widespread distribution of 'privilege' and 'property' was a dream beyond the reach of economically impoverished and politically marginalised Americans of all races. The breakdown of legal racial segregation and the allocation of citizenship rights to black Americans were the first and foremost objectives of MLK's anti-racist agenda – but a thorough examination of his public speeches demonstrates that he desired a radical redistribution of economic and political power. The Baptist minister promoted multi-racial forms of non-violent protest that aspired to benefit the poor of both races – black and white. Through mass non-violent action, MLK saw an opportunity to avoid a national disaster and create a new spirit of 'class and racial harmony'.

Speaking to a strong following in the city of Memphis in the southern state of Tennessee in March 1968, MLK warned that 'if America does not use her vast resources of wealth to end poverty and make it possible for all of God's children to have the basic necessities of life, she too will go to hell'.[5] This was at the heart of his 'Poor People's Campaign', which was in progress before his assassination. He dreamt of a politico-economic settlement whereby the problems of the poorest were placed at the heart of government thinking in the world's wealthiest nation – of a future underpinned by the values of justice, fair play and opportunity. He preached a traditional left-wing message of interracial social cohesion. Indeed, the best-known part of his 'I Have a Dream' speech, delivered at the Lincoln Memorial on 28 August 1963, is his vision of little black boys and girls joining hands with little white boys and girls as sisters and brothers in the southern state of Alabama. This is a far cry from the segregationist tendencies which have come to characterise contemporary racial identity politics in the West, as illustrated by 'safe spaces' along racial lines and proposed boycotts of non-black-owned businesses.

The toxic mixture of pseudo-intellectual race theories and racially motivated discrimination which increasingly defines modern leftist activism is very far removed from traditional MLK-style anti-racism. No one who is genuinely interested in cultivating stronger forms of social cohesion should focus exclusively on social class and ignore the impact of racial and cultural discrimination in the process. But one of the fundamental weaknesses of modern-day 'progressive activism' is the placing of racial discrimination at the heart of discussions of complex forms of social and economic disadvantage, thereby downplaying the effect of class-based barriers which threaten the personal advancement of underprivileged people of all races. This 'hyper-racialisation' of socio-economic inequalities threatens to trivialise the degree to which sections of the white-majority population are disadvantaged and anything but 'privileged'.

The grievance industry's continued efforts to frame racial and ethnic disparities as direct products of 'systemic racism' and 'structural discrimination' are unhelpful in understanding class-related disadvantages which can stymie the progress of working-class young people in diverse and deprived neighbourhoods. This includes a lack of contacts in 'higher-up' positions of society and the influence of 'old-boy networks' – informal all-male systems in which wealthy men with similar social and educational backgrounds help one another over business and personal matters. This can include facilitating employment and internship opportunities for the children of friends and acquaintances in the network. There is also some value in arguments which suggest that working-class communities in the regions – including in a string of multi-ethnic, post-industrial towns across northern England – have suffered chronic underinvestment for decades. This has left the UK with the most inter-regionally imbalanced economy in the industrialised world – one with a terribly unequal distribution of income. Indeed, the UK economy can be best described as an overly centralised one dominated by an individual city region in the shape of London (which happens to be the most racially diverse 'region', with a number of boroughs, such as Harrow and Croydon, having majority-non-white populations).

According to the Social Mobility Commission's 2019 poll, 77 per cent of people feel there is a large gap between the social classes in Britain today.[6] While Thatcherite diehards may simplistically label such a position a form of neo-Marxism, I suspect that there are a good number of traditional Tories within such a huge chunk of the population, which represents more than three in four people. While it has been argued that a degree of inequality generates a kind of envious aspiration that, in turn, turbocharges economic growth (I am personally no fan of the pursuit of equality of outcome), polling suggests that a booming majority of British people believe that the current state of affairs surrounding socio-economic inequality is unacceptable. This makes Labour's crushing defeat in the December 2019 general election all the more tragic – public anxieties over social-class inequalities are very much a mainstream feature of Britain. But if there is one message that this book of mine wants to send, it is this: 'culture' issues matter very much in this age of British politics (and beyond).

Despite the fact that 50 per cent of people believe that central government should be doing more to improve social mobility, socio-economic status is all too often left out of 'diversity' discussions.[7] Two young people with similar 'protected characteristics' are simply not on a level playing field if one belongs to an economically secure family and lives in a rapidly regenerating part of London, while the other belongs to a poverty-stricken family struggling to make ends meet in a relatively stagnant coastal town such as Blackpool. Many on the modern British left – including Labour frontbenchers such as Anneliese Dodds – are guilty of 'racialising' national problems such as our cost-of-living crisis. But skyrocketing energy bills and food prices will not only endanger the financial security of deprived black households in inner-city areas – they will also have a negative effect on poorer white households in the provinces. Research by the Yorkshire Building Society in 2021 – before the cost-of-living crisis gained a foothold – found that one in four Brits had less than £500 in savings.[8] The UK evidently has a savings crisis that cuts across many ethnic groups.

This is one of the fundamental weaknesses of the left: racialising complex outcomes and crudely framing them as structural racial inequalities. The Labour Party's importation of US-style racial-grievance politics – including the embrace of 'white privilege' theories – is both undermining its credibility in the British policy space and harming its appeal in the electoral marketplace. The UK is in desperate need of a traditional social-democratic party that understands the shared economic concerns and social anxieties of the multiracial working classes. What it doesn't need is an 'Americanised' activist organisation that continually fragments the British people on the grounds of race. This is something that I will tackle in Chapter 2, which focuses on the proliferation of racial identity politics in the modern Labour Party under one of its recent leaders.

Unfortunately, in the past few years we have witnessed homogenising and divisive concepts such as 'white culture', 'white oppression' and 'white privilege' become mainstream, in the process setting back British race relations. With 'ethnic-minority' and 'non-white' at times being lazily treated as synonyms, the performance of white ethnic minorities (such as people of Irish Traveller origin) tends to be ignored in the debate over ethnic disparities. I have been critical of the 'BAME' acronym – a dreadful and unhelpful umbrella term which lumps together vastly different ethnic groups, including people of Indian, Pakistani, Bangladeshi, black-Caribbean and black-African origin. But what is missing from broader discussions on race and culture is the degree of ethnic and cultural diversity within the UK's white population – masked by crude, one-size-fits-all CRT-inspired concepts.

One of my Punjabi elders in Luton once labelled our town's Irish Catholic community as 'white Sikhs'. Like many British Sikhs, many Irish Brits are hard-working, family-oriented and community-spirited; they value education and enjoy a good drink. I followed this up with a question about English people. 'A bit different,' he responded bluntly. Just as the general population has varying perceptions of different non-white groups, the same can be said for non-white Brits' perceptions of different white communities. While it is important not to give too much credence to sweeping generalisations, I can't help but feel that my Punjabi elder may have been on to something.

On a number of socio-economic indicators, Irish Brits fare better than the white-British mainstream. Data from 2021 shows that the average hourly pay for workers of Irish origin is £18.14, with the corresponding rate for white-British workers being £13.46.[9] The Irish are out-performing white Brits in education, too. The average 'Attainment 8' score (a mark out of 90 across eight GCSE-level qualifications) for white-British pupils in England in 2020–21 was 50.2 – this rose to 55.7 for pupils of white-Irish origin.[10] What could account for such differences? This is something I will flesh out in Chapter 7, when I dig deep into the drivers of educational and professional success of British ethnic minorities (and yes, Irish Brits represent an ethnic minority in their own right, despite their 'whiteness').

But we should not overlook the plight of Britain's Gypsy and Traveller communities, who are blighted by unstable family structures, poor educational outcomes and relatively high levels of criminal-justice involvement. Despite their relatively youthful profile, these communities did not fare well during the Covid-19 pandemic. Many live in confined households and are disproportionately affected by a lack of basic amenities, including running water and adequate sanitation and waste-management facilities. These white children living under such squalid conditions can hardly be described as the beneficiaries of race-based privilege – especially when one considers the broad 'acceptability' of anti-Gypsy and anti-Traveller bigotry in mainstream British society.

Such instances – the relatively high performance of Irish Catholic communities in the UK compared to the white-British mainstream and the material deprivation among Gypsies and Travellers – make a complete mockery of absurd catch-all terms like 'white privilege'. Contrary to what divisive identitarians would lead us to believe, Britain's white people are not a hyper-privileged, ethnically homogeneous bloc with a singular culture. Far from it. There are notable forms of cultural diversity within the UK's white population, and this in turn can feed into social and economic disparities between different ethnic groups. This is likely to be one of the main takeaways when the new 2021 census data is crunched over time. CRT and the associated concept of 'white privilege' are not only socially divisive, but form the basis of pseudo-intellectual ramblings which are increasingly being treated in a number of social institutions as incontestable fact.

In order to legitimise the theory of white privilege in the public space, we have seen desperate attempts to redefine 'racism' as solely rooted in 'power structures that uphold and perpetuate racism'. Supposedly 'anti-racist' academics and authors argue that white people cannot experience racism due to existing 'power dynamics' between different racial groups. All of this represents an aggressively racialised view of social structures in which white people are a powerful racial collective – and one that enjoys a basket of privileges over 'systemically oppressed' non-white people. It is precisely this kind of divisive interpretation of racism which is responsible for the worrying normalisation of anti-white bigotry on the British contemporary left.

No 'anti-racist' is worth the label unless they are willing to challenge and expose all forms of racism – irrespective of the backgrounds of the perpetrator and the victim. The conventional understanding of racism – prejudice, discrimination or antagonism by an individual, community or institution against a person or people on the basis of their membership of a particular racial group – should remain the cornerstone of anti-racist activism in the UK. However, such an approach has no place under new-age 'anti-racist' orthodoxy, as an acceptance of this definition ultimately involves recognising that white people have themselves been – and continue to be – victims of racism.

In October 2020, government minister and 'anti-woke' trailblazer Kemi Badenoch vigorously criticised the proliferation of white-privilege theories, calling them a dangerous trend in British race relations and stating that any school teaching them as fact was indeed breaking the law. However, Britain's merry band of 'diversity, equality and inclusion' professionals have a rather different view. Take, for example, the BBC's director of creative diversity, June Sarpong. Asserting that white privilege is a 'fact of life', Ms Sarpong added that, while the 'elite white male' is at the top of the tree, even the white working classes are advantaged over people of Asian and black backgrounds: 'You may be discriminated against because of class, you may be discriminated against because of your age, you may be discriminated against because of gender, size, etc., but you will never be discriminated against because of your race and that in itself feeds into the concept of white privilege.'[11]

It is clear that the concept of white privilege is far from being a matter of 'fact' – as the likes of Sarpong have claimed – when we consider how some police officials prioritised racial sensitivities over public safety when it came to certain cases of systematic child sexual abuse involving white-British girls and non-white men. And despite the 'white male' being seen as 'hyper-privileged' under intersectional frameworks, it is white working-class boys who are falling well behind in educational outcomes. Narratives of white privilege are also responsible for placing race at the forefront of disadvantage, when there are a range of other social factors – including family structure, community support and cultural attitudes towards education – which have a critical impact on life chances. The concept of 'white privilege' is an instrument predominantly used by white middle-class liberals to appear virtuous, while deflecting attention away from their own secure socio-economic position.

It is also used by non-white identitarian leftists to disguise problematic cultural norms which feed into minority forms of disadvantage. For example, we cannot ignore religio-cultural community views on gender roles when discussing the relatively low rates of female economic activity in Britain's Sylheti-origin population. Neither can we ignore relatively high levels of family breakdown and numbers of lone-parent households when considering the myriad social and economic problems concentrated in Britain's black-Caribbean communities. At the same time, it unhelpfully deflects attention away from meaningful sources of advantage – belonging to a stable family unit, aspirational parental attitudes, being part of a supportive local community – which have been somewhat eroded in the white-British mainstream but are firmly embedded in robust and thriving non-white groups such as Britain's Indian- and Chinese-origin minorities.

For those who still doubt the influence of identitarian leftist politics and the proliferation of white-privilege theories in our public institutions, look no further than the recent developments in our National Health Service. It is safe to say that the NHS did not cover itself in glory when, in September 2021, it published a blog post by Aishnine Benjamin, who is the 'equality, diversity and inclusion lead' at the Nursing and Midwifery Council, in which the author essentially told white people in the UK to 'educate' themselves about their racial 'privilege' and 'fragility' – an instruction unlikely to go down well in predominantly white, left-behind, post-industrial communities with struggling health and social-care systems. Addressing all white people in the UK as if they were a hyper-privileged racial collective, she wrote: 'You don't have to be vocal but do "listen". Listening means being open to hearing what black and minority ethnic people are saying.'[12]

This was followed later in the same month by *The Telegraph*'s disclosure that NHS England staff are being offered training on the BLM movement. New 'diversity courses' available for NHS health and care staff cover 'white privilege', unconscious bias and 'authentic ally-ship'. One of the online courses is on the history, guiding principles and key messages of the controversial BLM movement, with a link to an interview with its founders. BLM is described in the course as a 'healing' movement that works to 'eradicate white supremacy' and whose 'prime focus is to expose and challenge anti-blackness in its multiple manifestations'. Medical professionals are encouraged to examine NHS policies through the prism of BLM ideological thinking, as this will supposedly be useful in 'fuelling' better 'racial equity' in our healthcare system.[13] This latest diversity drive has occurred despite the then health secretary, Sajid Javid, telling parliamentarians that he would be 'watchful for any waste or wokery' from the NHS following the tax hike to boost funding for healthcare services.[14]

I consider myself to be an anti-racist of the traditional left, but there is nothing that can convince me that these kinds of pro-BLM initiatives will help to foster the development of a more culturally responsive and socially inclusive healthcare system. The reality of the matter is that the BLM movement is not one that commands broad-based public support. Indeed, there is an existing body of polling which shows that notable sections of the British population think that BLM has destabilised race relations in the UK. The idea that a publicly funded healthcare service should be guided by the 'principles' of a social movement which has been responsible for sowing the seeds of division is utterly unacceptable.

There are marginalised sections of the British population who face social and cultural barriers when it comes to accessing crucial healthcare services. Local NHS trusts – especially in diverse urban localities – need to develop strong relationships with well-respected civic organisations that can act as 'connectors' to traditionally distrustful communities. The Covid-19 pandemic has exposed the fact that tailored health-awareness interventions for different communities are required when coordinating wider public-health responses. This should be the bread-and-butter work for NHS professionals in the 'equality and inclusion' sphere. But the NHS's bloated layer of 'inclusion professionals' and their implementation of BLM-inspired 'diversity initiatives' will achieve very little in terms of serving the broader public interest. Managerial classes channelling BLM would do better to create practical solutions to address the conditions affecting ethnic minorities. We must not allow imported race theories to take hold within our healthcare system. Pushing back on social activists who are responsible for neglecting the basics, as well as fomenting racial division, should be a public-policy priority for the current government.

And we should not overlook the reality that there are vital health disparities which demonstrate the limitations of white-privilege theories. For instance, white men – often presented by the modern left as the most advantaged section of British society – have one of the lowest rates of life expectancy.[15] Furthermore, existing survey data shows that, when compared with Asian and black racial categories, white Brits are more likely to say that they have had suicidal thoughts. They are also more likely to say that they have carried out suicide attempts and acts of self-harm.[16] These racial and ethnic disparities relating to life expectancy and mental well-being are all too often overlooked.

Alongside the peddling of racial identity politics in our publicly funded healthcare system, there is a real worry over the degree to which supposed 'educationalists' are abusing their position of authority by promoting such ideas in the classroom – hoping to mould young, impressionable minds through their in-school political activism. The extent to which teaching resources inspired by the BLM movement are being hosted by online platforms such as *Times Education Supplement* (*Tes*) and the Chartered College of Teaching is something that understandably gives rise to the view that, in many of our institutions, there are far too many who are exploiting their level of power and influence to spread American-inspired race theories – and neglecting their most basic of duties in the process. Schools should act as intellectual hubs that promote self-discipline and foster healthy ties between pupils from all walks of life. As well as equipping young people with the knowledge and skills they need to thrive in adulthood, state schools – especially in multiracial neighbourhoods – should play an integral role in cultivating forms of mutual understanding and respect. Presenting racially divisive concepts such as white privilege as fact heightens the risk of racial BLM-style self-segregation taking place in our schools, which has the potential to undermine social cohesion in the long term.

However, there is evidence that the socio-cultural backlash to the infiltration of racial identitarian activists in the sphere of schooling is under way. In June 2021 the (genuinely) anti-racist campaigning group Don't Divide Us (DDU) launched a petition opposing the Green Party-led Brighton and Hove City Council's plans to provide state-funded schoolteachers with 'anti-racism' training based on CRT. Green councillor Hannah Clare, the chair of the council's Children, Young People and Skills Committee, was quoted in the local media as saying: 'Critical race theory is our lens for developing our understanding of the complexities of racism – and not an ideology.'[17] A draft version of the council's 'anti-racist schools strategy' stated that 'racial literacy training' would be required for all staff, and that, instead of taking a 'colour-blind approach', they would gain an understanding of 'structural/systemic racism'. There would be a 'move away from a Eurocentric approach' to teaching, with the aim of 'diversifying and decolonising the curriculum'.[18]

The DDU petition has attracted thousands of signatories from all walks of British life.

We should not be in any doubt about this: CRT is a crudely simplistic and deeply divisive theory of American origin that is being promoted to encourage feelings of anti-system victimhood in Britain – one of the fairest and least discriminatory places on earth. The concept of white privilege ultimately encourages white pupils to feel like 'oppressors' and their black peers to feel like 'the oppressed'. This kind of toxicity has no place in Britain's multiracial society and is especially unfair on aspirational ethnic-minority parents who believe that there are plenty of opportunities for their children to thrive and progress in their own country.

There have occasionally been signs that the current Conservative government is beginning to smell the coffee. In October 2021 the then education secretary Nadhim Zahawi made it clear that the concept of 'white privilege' should not be presented as fact in schools. He declared that pupils should not be exposed to contested theories such as this in the classroom without appropriate balance being provided. Zahawi's robust intervention – the first time in a generation that a government minister has intervened over teachers' political impartiality in the school system – came after the publication of the Education Select Committee's report that urged schools to cease using the phrase 'white privilege', advancing the view that it 'pits one group against another'. But I would argue that the Tory government has not tackled the issue as robustly as it should have.

Another possible indication of the government's awareness of the problem was the appointment of Katharine Birbalsingh CBE as the chair of the Social Mobility Commission in October 2021, a move that, unsurprisingly, ruffled feathers. The hard-nosed founder and headmistress of the high-achieving Michaela Community School has established herself as one of the most influential educationalists in Britain. The Wembley-based free school has a strong, traditional emphasis on discipline and order – adopting a zero-tolerance policy towards poor behaviour. In May 2017, it was rated 'outstanding' in all categories by Ofsted. Birbalsingh certainly has a proven track record when it comes to going against the socially liberal grain. Indeed, her nonconformist contributions in the sphere of education saw her being awarded the Contrarian Prize in 2019. Birbalsingh's appointment was a bitter blow to all those who simplistically place racial identity at the heart of discussions on complex forms of social and economic disadvantage. However, she stepped down from her role after just one year – arguing that the media portrayal of her 'controversial' opinions was jeopardising the Cabinet Office body's work.

In recent times, the social-policy space has seen the acceleration of reductive narratives that fail to appreciate the myriad factors that collectively determine life chances in modern-day Britain. As was pointed out in a report published in March 2021 by the Commission on Race and Ethnic Disparities (CRED), many of Britain's South Asian and black-African communities – across different socio-economic classes – are deeply family-oriented and intergenerationally cohesive.[19] Academic excellence in many cases is relentlessly promoted in the household. Civic associations within such communities continue to flourish, helping to provide a spiritually uplifting sense of belonging and rootedness. In my own case, whether it was at the local newsagents or the Asian greengrocer's, my community elders would take an interest in how I was performing at school, college and university. Not only does this make a young person feel valued, it provides a healthy pressure, motivating young people not to disappoint their own parents, as well as to avoid potential embarrassment in the wider local community.

The unfortunate reality is that too many coastal and former industrial towns have seen the collapse of the family unit and the disintegration of local communities. As far back as 2013, research from the Centre for Social Justice (CSJ) found that children who experienced family breakdown were twice as likely to fail at school.[20] Against a backdrop of substance misuse and alcohol dependency, responsible and inspiring adult role models are relatively scarce. This is the story of predominantly white 'left behind' coastal towns – whether it is Blackpool in Lancashire or Great Yarmouth in Norfolk. But the same goes for deprived white-majority neighbourhoods in cities such as Nottingham, Sheffield, Stoke-on-Trent or Hull. These parts of the country are not only materially deprived, but also socially atomised and spiritually disconnected. And it is safe to say that 'white privilege' is not in high supply in these disadvantaged inner-city neighbourhoods, coastal areas and post-industrial towns – they contain some of the most underprivileged communities in Britain.

The problem with many left-leaning progressive liberals who are eager to 'represent' ethnic-minority 'concerns' is that they refuse to acknowledge the complex range of factors which feed into certain disparities in modern-day Britain. And reductive white-privilege theories are severely limited in explaining such ethnic differences. Tuning in to BBC2's *Newsnight* one night in July 2021, I watched policy editor Lewis Goodall provide a five-minute examination of 'structural racism' in Britain. This included looking at the representation of ethnic minorities in public institutions and the differences in average household assets between groups. A clip of the segment went viral on social media, winning the approval of Twitter's army of social-justice warriors. But Goodall's piece failed to consider a myriad of social and cultural factors at play when dissecting the racial-disparity figures.

It is true that South Asians are 'under-represented' and whites are 'over-represented' in Britain's police forces. But, as former Surrey police and crime commissioner Kevin Hurley has observed, the decision to join the police is often a 'family affair'. Mainstream policing recruitment is partly driven by a willingness to follow in the footsteps of relatives who have already served. We might compare this to the way in which Indian-origin parents are renowned for encouraging their children to work towards white-collar professional roles – especially in sectors such as healthcare and finance. While police forces could invest more in 'diversifying' their intake, these family and community dynamics should not be ignored. Nor should we overlook the fact that, according to a recent study from the campaign group Hope Not Hate, a comfortable majority (64 per cent) of ethnic-minority Britons believe the police are, on the whole, a force for good, and that racism in policing is down to a small number of problematic individuals.[21] Needless to say, these counter-arguments did not feature in Goodall's segment. Levels of institutional trust which expose the modern left's simplistic caricaturing of ethnic minorities as some sort of disillusioned, grievance-riddled bloc is something I discuss in greater detail in Chapter 6.

The roles played by migratory background and socio-cultural practices were also ignored in Goodall's discussion of wealth disparities. The trajectory of each ethnic-minority group is heavily influenced by the resources of the first generation who arrived in Britain. Well-educated migrants with sound business acumen tend to provide strong foundations for future generational advancement. Bangladeshi households, as Goodall points out, have some of the lowest asset levels in Britain. But the majority of British Bangladeshis originally migrated from deprived rural villages, particularly from the Sylhet region. And the Bangladeshi population is residentially concentrated in London – an expensive city to live in, making wealth accumulation that bit harder. What's more, conservative gender norms have led to Bangladeshi women having much larger families and lower levels of economic activity.

One of the most significant disparities in Britain is in family structure and fatherlessness – a glaring omission from Goodall's *Newsnight* piece. Recent Office for National Statistics (ONS) data shows that only 6 per cent of British Indian dependants up to the age of 15 years live in a lone-parent household. This rises to an astonishing 63 per cent for their peers of black-Caribbean origin.[22] Considering that two-parent households are strongly associated with a range of positive outcomes – such as educational attainment, mental well-being and cognitive development – these kinds of ethnic-group differences in family dynamics cannot be brushed under the carpet when discussing economic and social disparities. Too many progressives insist that disparities must mean discrimination – or that only 'structural racism' can be to blame.

Unfortunately, this has fundamentally undermined the seriousness of Labour Party discussions of important matters of social justice – such as child poverty. Research produced by the party that was released in January 2022 found notable racial and ethnic disparities in child-poverty rates. The findings were certainly stark. More than half of black children in the UK are growing up in poverty (53 per cent) – compared to only 26 per cent of their white peers.[23] However, the analysis failed to provide ethnic-group breakdowns within the broader racial groups – meaning that child-poverty levels among white Gypsies and Travellers of Irish descent were left unreported, as were the difference in child-poverty rates between people of black-Caribbean origin and their co-racial counterparts of African heritage.

Overall, 27 per cent of all children in the UK were living in poor households in 2010–11, compared to 31 per cent now.[24] Shadow women and equalities secretary Anneliese Dodds, whose office produced the new analysis, said: 'Conservative incompetence and denialism about the existence of structural racism are driving black children into poverty.'[25] The answer, she claimed, is a 'new race equality act to tackle structural racial inequality at source'. Dr Halima Begum, chief executive of racial-equality think tank the Runnymede Trust – and no stranger to making woeful statements on British race relations – said the figures were 'cause for considerable concern' and that 'Black children face racism and poverty'.[26]

But while Labour is keen to discuss 'structural inequalities' that underpin the very mixed picture of prosperity in Britain, the party seems altogether warier of two profoundly important factors: family and culture. Discussing ethnic differences in family structure and cultural norms may not fit in with the identitarian script when it comes to child poverty, but they are undoubtedly influential in such outcomes. Three in ten children in the UK live in poverty. This rises to one in two for children living in lone-parent households.[27]

There is also a link between family size and child poverty. According to the Joseph Rowntree Foundation, for the year 2019–20, the child-poverty rate for two-child households was 24 per cent – this almost doubled, to 47 per cent, for households with three or more children.[28] While it may not be politically correct, it is time that family structure was placed at the heart of our national child-poverty debate. As discussed, there are other factors that can feed into higher-than-mainstream child-poverty rates – such as cultural barriers to female economic activity and certain groups being relatively concentrated in ultra-competitive London (with its high-cost economy and dysfunctional housing market). But I suspect that residential distribution is not quite as 'fashionable' as 'systemic racism' when it comes to explaining ethnic disparities in child-poverty rates.

Moving on to the world of sport, one of the most significant developments of 2021 was the racism scandal involving British Pakistani cricketer Azeem Rafiq and Yorkshire County Cricket Club (CCC). Rafiq, who accused the club of 'institutional racism' and English cricket of being 'institutionally racist', gave evidence in Parliament to the Digital, Culture, Media and Sport Select Committee in November and was championed as an anti-racist 'trailblazer' by the BBC – before he ended up having to apologise for historical anti-Semitic comments made on social media.[29] There was one particular statistic that did the rounds in the British media: while three in ten players in recreational/club cricket are of South Asian origin, this drops to just 4 per cent in the county game.[30] While this was considered to be evidence of widespread institutional racism in English cricket, interventions made by prominent British Asian cricketers suggest that this is an oversimplified explanation which ignores the role of personal agency and the attitudes towards the sport of sceptical parents – who view it as a high-risk career choice that is unlikely to provide long-term economic stability.

Huddersfield-born and Bradford-raised Ajmal Shahzad – the first British-born Asian to play for Yorkshire, who has represented England in all three formats of the game (Test, 50-over and Twenty20) – commented about the difficulty of combining employment and a sporting career:

> When you get to a certain age and you need to earn money from work, something's got to give and some of the time they go on and do office jobs and sacrifice sport... some people can't just play cricket in the hope that they are going to get paid or make it as a professional.[31]

Nottinghamshire's Samit Patel – who, like Shahzad, has represented England in all three versions of the game – has suggested that part of the answer lies in the career expectations of some British Asian parents: 'I don't think they take cricket that seriously, they think cricket doesn't make the money they think, they'd rather their son or daughter be a doctor or a dentist, or something like that.'[32] Of course, it's no surprise that their voices have not been mainstreamed – their nuanced and balanced approach to the 'diversity, equality and inclusion' debate in cricket does not suit the 'progressive' identitarian narrative.

There is a discussion to be had on how we can foster more inclusive and culturally sensitive dressing rooms at various levels of English cricket. This includes exploring how English drinking culture can potentially alienate young, gifted British Muslim players who have aspirations to represent their own county and country. And there is certainly no denying that a rotten culture was allowed to take root at Yorkshire CCC – one that enabled and encouraged discrimination against Asian players. However, if we are to examine topics of accessibility and ethnic-minority representation in the higher levels of the sport, it is vital that we do not lock ourselves into the reductive 'disparities = discrimination' paradigm. The prioritisation of academic commitments and culturally driven career decisions should be considered potential factors when exploring why young and talented players of South Asian origin don't end up becoming professional cricketers.

Even in the one area where the notion of 'white privilege' could hold some weight, its usefulness is somewhat limited. An example of this is the discourse surrounding CV-based field experiments which show that, after controlling for qualifications, skills and work experience, applications with 'culturally distant' names fare worse than those with traditionally 'English-sounding' names across a range of sectors in the UK economy. This is something that has been highlighted a great deal by the director of the British Future think tank, Sunder Katwala. This would naturally place a comfortable majority of the UK's white population at an advantage and much of the non-white population at a disadvantage. Recent reports published by institutions such as the Centre for Social Investigation (CSI) at Nuffield College, University of Oxford, have shown that this has a particularly strong effect on applicants from Muslim-majority countries of origin – especially those in South Asia, the Middle East, North Africa and the Horn of Africa (including Somalia).[33] I myself have long been supportive of the expansion of name-blind CV initiatives across the public, private and third sectors; indeed, it was something I recommended in my PhD thesis, published in 2019.[34]

But if it is the case that traditionally English-sounding names fare better in such processes than more 'culturally distant' ones, then surely a black-Caribbean-origin applicant named 'John Campbell' would be at an advantage when compared with a white, Lithuanian-origin applicant named 'Egidijus Kuzminskas'? And if Muslim-sounding names fare badly in CV-based field experiments, does that also apply to white Muslim applicants from the Balkans – such as 'Sead Muslimović'? Even in the case of classic 'CV discrimination' exercises, it is not simply a matter of 'black and white'. And some ethnic minorities may be disproportionately impacted by such forms of name-based discrimination compared to others – including white ones. We mustn't forget the

Pontins 'undesirable guest blacklist' – a register of 'suspect' surnames that, according to the conclusions of the Equality and Human Rights Commission (EHRC), was designed to discriminate against members of the Gypsy and Traveller communities.[35] One of the key problems with 'white privilege' and the view that discrimination is a 'majority-on-minorities' enterprise is that they overlook forms of intra-group prejudice within the overall white and non-white populations. This is not a mature anti-racist approach to take if one is genuinely serious about fighting discrimination and bolstering social cohesion in twenty-first-century Britain.

Discrimination and prejudice are not straightforward 'black and white' issues. They can exist within the same racial category – indeed, within the same ethnic group (and that certainly includes Britain's ethnic minorities, where issues surrounding colourism persist). To tackle the sources of discrimination, we must not be selective. As well as doing away with this kind of 'anti-racism selectivity', the proliferation of white-privilege theories across Britain's public institutions must be challenged.

All too often imported from US 'educational' institutions which are increasingly becoming dogmatic hubs of race-obsessed activity, theoretical frameworks which 'racialise' deprivation and disadvantage will not serve our multiracial democracy well. Discrimination has now established itself as a catch-all explanation for complex racial and ethnic disparities – with important socio-cultural factors such as family structure, parental support, community dynamics and neighbourhood-level assets being left unacceptably by the wayside. And some of the greatest problems surrounding family breakdown and social atomisation are in those predominantly white communities that are deprived of meaningful educational and business investment and are lacking in wholesome civic assets that can provide young people with a sense of local pride and belonging.

While much of the British left obsesses with protected characteristics – from sexual orientation to gender reassignment – class barely features in its analyses of social inequalities. Even worse, the undeniable importance of family structure in shaping life chances is treated as an inconvenience by 'racial-justice warriors'. The end result is not only that embedded forms of disadvantage in predominantly white-British communities are overlooked, but also that, depressingly, uplifting stories of ethnic-minority educational success and socio-economic advancement are hidden. Indeed, there is a growing suspicion that much of the modern British left is reluctant to champion upward mobility among non-white minorities as it threatens to undercut their precious white-privilege narratives and their perception of Britain as a hellish island of rampant institutional racism. This is the doom-and-gloom identitarian narrative-setting which reigns supreme on the modern British left – including in the Labour Party, which finds itself in thrall to racial identity politics.

2

LABOUR'S IDENTITY-
POLITICS PROBLEM

There was a time when the Labour Party was the leading anti-discrimination force in mainstream British
politics. Effective race-relations legislation, designed to
promote the economic, social and political integration
of ethnic minorities, was passed under successive Labour
governments: the party established the Equality and
Human Rights Commission (EHRC) in 2007, under
Tony Blair's leadership, and passed the 2010 Equality Act
under Gordon Brown. The 2010 Act, designed to provide
legal protection from discrimination in the workplace
and wider society, consolidated a set of protected characteristics which included ethnicity and religious belief.
It was this steadfast commitment to anti-discrimination
that made Labour my natural party. Being a British man
of Bangladeshi and Uttarpradeshi Muslim heritage, I felt
they were 'my team'.

I voted for Labour in both the 2010 and the 2015 UK general elections. I remember how anxious I felt about the prospect of the small-state alliance of Cameronian Tories and 'Orange Booker' Liberal Democrats cutting public funds for Labour-voting working-class towns such as mine to the bone. I have always been of the view that Luton is a place defined by its belief in the practical power of on-the-ground social conservatism and well-crafted government intervention. In this sense, the Conservative–Liberal Democrat coalition was a nightmarish government for many Lutonians. The Cameron–Clegg axis of economic and social liberalism, with community-ripping austerity and the prioritisation of the individual at the heart of it, did not remotely appeal to my communitarian and protectionist instincts.

On the night of the 2015 general election, I had a lads' dinner at a local Thai. I was in an optimistic mood – Ed Miliband may well have been unable to eat a bacon sarnie without looking like the most awkward man on earth, but I believed that Labour could at least manage to become the largest party in Parliament. By the time the exit-poll results were delivered, I had polished off my chicken massaman curry and jasmine rice with aplomb – I even treated myself to a 'Phuket Island' for dessert (green pancakes filled with desiccated coconut, served with vanilla ice cream – I highly recommend it). I could scarcely believe the projection: the Tories would continue to be the largest parliamentary party, with Labour's number of seats falling. In fact, the

Conservatives – who managed to win a million ethnic-minority voters for the first time – ended up with an outright parliamentary majority, taking their junior coalition partner to the cleaners in the south-west of England. Meanwhile, senior Labour shadow cabinet members, notably Ed Balls and Douglas Alexander, along with Scottish Labour leader Jim Murphy, were defeated in their constituencies. Whether I liked it or not, the Tories had managed to win over aspirational voters – including those in Gujarati Hindu and Punjabi Sikh families – who were economically self-sufficient, not necessarily reliant on benefits and put off by Labour's interventionist policies designed to support the replenishment of the all-encompassing welfare state.

The Labour Party – and the broader left – was understandably hurting a great deal. Some believed that Ed Miliband was guilty of appeasement when it came to Tory-led austerity – that a more ambitious 'anti-austerity' stance was needed instead of meek soft-leftism. A radical backlash was inevitable. In the 2015 party-leadership contest, four MPs were nominated: Andy Burnham, Yvette Cooper, Liz Kendall and the hard-left, perennially rebellious backbencher Jeremy Corbyn. Growing support for Corbyn, who entered the race as the left-field (in every sense), 'dark-horse' candidate, combined with the release of numerous opinion polls that showed him in the lead, led to high-profile interventions by a number of prominent New Labour figures, including Tony Blair, Gordon Brown, Alastair Campbell, Jack Straw and David

Miliband, arguing that Corbyn's election as leader would leave the party unelectable.

For a party membership dominated by those who believed that the New Labour project ultimately adopted the core tenets of Thatcherite, neo-liberal orthodoxy and dragged the country into an illegal foreign military campaign in Iraq, such interventions only served to solidify – if not grow – pro-Corbyn sentiments. In September 2015, Corbyn was elected in the first round, receiving 59.5 per cent of the vote. Another leadership contest was held a year later, following internal discontent over Corbyn's approach to the Remain campaign in the June 2016 referendum on EU membership. It was clear as day that Corbyn belonged to the left-wing Eurosceptic tradition that views the EU as a neo-liberal project which enriches the transnational capitalist classes through the commodification of the poor. Corbyn defeated sole challenger Owen Smith by 61.8 per cent to 38.2 per cent – with his comfortable victory in the head-to-head contest further strengthening his authority as party leader.

One of the scarier elements of Corbynism was its cult-like nature. Corbyn could do no wrong – he was a political messiah who was morally infallible. Treated as some kind of modern-day prophet representing all-round virtue and righteousness, his performance in the 2017 general election was treated by the faithful as some sort of victory. While the Tories under Theresa May were deprived of a parliamentary majority, Labour still finished 2.4 percentage points and 55 seats behind them. In the build-up to this 'victory', Corbyn tweeted what was some of the most patronising nonsense imaginable: 'Only Labour can be trusted to unlock the talent of Black, Asian and Minority Ethnic people, who have been held back by the Conservatives. We will guarantee equality is at the heart of our programme for government.'[1]

At this point, I had voted in two general elections – both times for Labour. But to be told by a mediocre, white-British politician that only his party could be trusted to 'unlock the talent' of people like me was something I did not take kindly to at all – and I suspect that I am not alone in that. It takes a certain form of arrogance – a grossly inflated sense of self-importance – to deliver such a hyper-paternalistic statement. Irrespective of who is governing the country, there are intelligent, hard-working and resilient ethnic-minority people across Britain who are perfectly able to utilise their abilities and smarts to move ahead in life – without the assistance of the supposedly 'talent-unlocking' Jeremy Corbyn. I would trust ethnic-minority parents, grandparents, community elders, dedicated educators and youth-outreach workers well before the likes of him and much of the opposition Labour Party when it comes to facilitating youth personal development. And while I have been far from impressed by the Conservatives over the lengthy period of their rule, many aspirational ethnic-minority Brits have managed to do quite well in the post-2010 period, with some shifting their allegiance from Labour to the Tories. Family support, community belonging, personal initiative and strategic life-planning hold the key to unlocking such talent – not a losing political organisation that had lifted a politician from far-left backbench mediocrity to the status of leader of (what was then) Her Majesty's Opposition.

From a social-cohesion perspective, the Corbyn years will be defined by Labour's identitarian toxification – the twin viruses of racial- and religious-minority politics coursed through the veins of a political party whose traditions are rooted in solidarity. The Labour Party should ultimately be an alliance-building vehicle for meaningful social and economic change – creating a wide progressive consensus that is unrelentingly focused on the standard of living for the working people of Britain, especially those who have suffered from stagnant wages, skyrocketing housing costs and crumbling public services. But while Corbyn did talk about economic unfairness in modern-day Britain, much of this was undone by problematic cultural developments under his leadership. The fetishisation of identity politics, combined with obfuscation on Brexit and the seeming inability to deal with its internal anti-Semitism crisis, meant that Labour was far detached from the desire for cultural security that ran through its traditional provincial and post-industrial heartlands – and it paid a heavy price for this in the 2019 general election.

Labour's fraternisation with academics, organisations and institutions with a fundamentally warped view of Britain escalated under Corbyn – who has never hesitated to express his solidarity with those who are not remotely interested in fostering a more cohesive and harmonious society. Momentum, a pro-Corbyn political organisation that was formed in the aftermath of his ascent to the leadership, dedicated itself to taking control of key bodies within the party's policy-creating and decision-making infrastructure, including the ruling National Executive Committee (NEC). Becoming a dominant force within the party, Momentum helped to produce a disastrous policy agenda that married open-borders cosmopolitanism with the aggressive prioritisation of minority-group interests. Outrider media organisations like Novara Media have also caused significant damage to Labour, appearing to have a fundamental loathing for patriotic, traditional working-class voters. (Take, for example, Aaron Bastani's denunciation of the Poppy Appeal.[2]) Such entities exploited Labour, using it as a vehicle to infiltrate mainstream politics and push ideas which were never going to be popular in England's quietly traditional, post-industrial districts and provincial market towns – places Labour needs in order to govern with a workable parliamentary majority.

One of Labour's central problems is that the self-labelled 'anti-racists' of the modern left, fuelled by aggressive racial (and religious) identity politics, appear reluctant to acknowledge that some of the most deprived communities in the UK are predominantly white. Britain's core cities, such as London and Birmingham, have their fair share of deprived, ethnically diverse constituencies. But there is also a large number of disadvantaged communities in ex-industrial and coastal towns that are far less diverse. A responsible party of the left – a practical, progressive political outfit – would be able to develop a policy agenda capable of commanding high levels of support across all of these constituencies. But many in and around the Labour Party are so utterly obsessed with 'white privilege' that they cannot even begin to feel any sense of affection towards underprivileged white-British people – including those who belong to families that have voted for Labour over generations.

This animus runs deep. White working-class people in the provinces are considered to be an inconvenience. And if these people dare to express a dissenting opinion – such as on Brexit – they can expect a volley of verbal abuse from the increasingly intolerant modern left: 'racist', 'thick', 'bigoted', 'jingoistic' and 'Little Englander' have become common slurs. The growth of identity politics within the Labour Party has given rise to a certain anti-white hatred – with the intersectional 'oppression pyramid' viewing white males as a hyper-advantaged section of British society. (This is anything but the case, especially when it comes to family structure and educational progress.)

Labour's publication of a separate 'Race and Faith' manifesto during the 2019 election was racial and religious identity politics at its peak.[3] It included proposals such as a race-equality unit in the Treasury to review the impact of all spending commitments on 'BAME communities'.

But there are many constituencies – both predominantly white and ethnically diverse – that have been starved of meaningful public investment for decades. Instead of its 'Race and Faith' initiative, Labour should have produced a 'Rebuilding Our Communities' manifesto, laying out an ambitious post-Brexit agenda based on local economic regeneration and decentralisation of political control. Policy initiatives such as town-centre regeneration and expansion of free ports, placed in the hands of those with local expertise and specialist knowledge, and accountable to their communities, could have been part of a broad post-Brexit plan to revive deprived parts of the country.

The 'Race and Faith' manifesto also reaffirmed the party's adoption of the working definition of 'Islamophobia' used by the All-Party Parliamentary Group on British Muslims.[4] As a British Muslim academic with a background in social cohesion, I can confidently say that this definition amounted to the creation of an identitarian blasphemy law through the back door. Of course, it is absolutely essential that anti-Muslim hatred and prejudice, which directly impact the well-being of British Muslims, are addressed. This includes anti-Muslim acts of hatred and violence – something we must take seriously when we consider that far-right extremism is the fastest-growing terror threat in the UK. More also needs to be done to tackle anti-Muslim prejudice in the UK labour market and the private rented-housing sector. But this spectacularly flawed definition has the potential to undermine our counterterrorism efforts. Worse, it represents a fundamental attack on free speech and robust intellectual enquiry. This is perhaps unsurprising, as modern-left 'academivists', who often prioritise the aggressive promotion of their regressive politics over rigorous academic investigation, were involved in the development of the definition. According to its terms, 'Islamophobia' includes 'accusing Muslim citizens of being more loyal to the "Ummah" (transnational Muslim community) or to their countries of origin, or to the alleged priorities of Muslims worldwide, than to the interests of their own nations'.[5] This section of the working definition strikes me, a researcher by trade, as deeply complicated from an academic perspective. British-based academics ought to be free to conduct research into British Muslims' identities and sense of belonging without facing the prospect of being accused of 'Islamophobia'. This is vitally important work, from a national cohesion point of view. But this definition risks making it very difficult. It is worth noting that a survey carried out by ICM Unlimited in the build-up to the 2019 general election found that more than four in ten British Muslims believed their co-religionist compatriots tended to be more loyal to Saudi Arabia (home to the holy cities of Makkah and Medina) than to the UK.[6] Under this definition, would they even have the freedom to express such a view?

The working definition dangerously conflates genuine anti-Muslim prejudice with perfectly reasonable criticism of orthodox religious doctrines and their social implications. As well as undermining academic freedom and suppressing intellectual openness, it harms the cause of minorities who are internally victimised by orthodox elements of the broader British Muslim population. Leading anti-female genital mutilation (FGM) and women's rights campaigner Nimco Ali has argued that the working definition would leave secular and feminist Muslim women vulnerable to being slandered as 'Islamophobic', as they seek to uphold the basic human rights and freedoms of women and question male interpretations of holy text.[7]

It would empower those who support patriarchal coercion, extremist practices and ultra-conservative gender roles within minority communities across the country. For instance, it would enable reactionary elements of Britain's Muslim population, providing them with a means to clamp down on important debates that offend their Islamist tendencies. In doing so, the definition would disempower and marginalise progressive Muslims who are trying to expose extremist behaviour and attitudes within their own religious communities. This would be an absolute win for misogynists and a major setback for the Muslim women who bravely stand up to them. It is extraordinary that MPs are the ones who came up with this.

At the heart of the issue is that Labour have been responsible for fraternising with, and at times praising, identitarian organisations which are anything but representative. Take, for example, the Islamic Human Rights Commission (IHRC), which, on its website, refers to itself as 'an independent campaign, research and advocacy NGO that struggles for justice for all peoples regardless of their racial, confessional or political background'.[8] One of its aims and objectives is to promote 'a new social and international order, based on truth, justice, righteousness and generosity, rather than selfish interest'.[9] According to media reports, Massoud Shadjareh, chair of the British-based IHRC, praised the fatwa on Sir Salman Rushdie when speaking at a conference on 'Islamophobia' – a year before the award-winning author was stabbed by a pro-Iran Shia extremist at a literary festival in New York.[10] And, prior to this, Shadjareh reportedly praised the late Ayatollah Khomeini as a 'torch of light for the whole of mankind'.[11]

The IHRC is also known for organising the annual Al-Quds Day march in London. At past events, speakers have glorified Ayatollah Khomeini, while protestors have expressed support for Hezbollah – the Lebanese Shia Islamist political party which calls for the destruction of the state of Israel and is proscribed in the UK. At one Al-Quds parade, held just a few days after the tragic Grenfell Tower fire in west London in 2017, Nazim Ali – an IHRC director – tried to blame 'Zionists' for the tragedy. 'It is the Zionists who give money to the Tory Party, to kill people in high-rise blocks,' he reportedly said.[12] How exactly this fits in with the IHRC's stated aim of promoting a truth-based social order is rather unclear. Dr Paul Stott, head of security and extremism at the think tank Policy Exchange, has concluded that the

IHRC is 'perhaps the most consistently pro-Iranian voice in London'.[13] The organisation has lots to say in relation to 'Islamophobia' in Britain, but little or nothing to say about the many well-documented human-rights abuses in the Islamic Republic of Iran. What does the Press TV-loving Jeremy Corbyn think of the IHRC? He once described the organisation as representing 'all that's best in Islam'.[14]

Corbyn's glowing endorsement of the IHRC – which has previously been referred to by the Henry Jackson Society think tank as an 'institutionally pro-terrorist and anti-Semitic organisation'[15] – encapsulated two somewhat intertwined problems for Labour under his tenure: its cosy relationship with identitarian, religio-political organisations and its institutional anti-Semitism crisis. As Labour's internal structures – including the NEC – were steadily 'colonised' by social-justice activists both tribalistic and reductionist in their world view, the balance of emphasis within the party shifted from broad-based social solidarity to divisive identity politics. But what was especially sinister under the leadership of Jeremy Corbyn was the ascent within the party of anti-capitalist tendencies and anti-Western foreign-policy approaches which sought to legitimise forms of anti-Semitism.

Irrespective of socio-economic status, Jewish communities at large have been subjected to the political mainstreaming of anti-Semitic beliefs. Popularised notions of 'Jewish privilege' in modern left-wing circles meant that there was – and continues to be – a lack of 'progressive solidarity' with British Jews over anti-Semitism. On the so-called 'oppression pyramid', Jews – due to their relative educational and economic success – are not viewed as a 'victimised' group. Due to the socio-economic status of particular groups, certain forms of discrimination are prioritised over others – with anti-Semitism ranking far below anti-Muslim prejudice or anti-black racism (something that is especially problematic when one considers that anti-Jewish conspiratorial beliefs are more prevalent in British Muslim and black-British communities than among the general population).

Yet Corbyn allowed this kind of thinking to fester in the Labour Party under his stewardship. His election as leader will forever be a stain on modern British political history. Labour was once a natural party for many of Britain's Jews. But Jewish politicians such as Luciana Berger and Dame Louise Ellman – MP for Liverpool Riverside for 22 years and a Labour member for 55 years – left the party due to anti-Semitism. (Both have now returned under the leadership of Sir Keir Starmer.) Before Labour's disastrous performance in the 2019 general election, a survey by Survation revealed that four in ten British Jews would seriously consider leaving the UK if Corbyn became prime minister.[16] It is quite astonishing that nearly half of an entire religious minority – one that has contributed so much to various spheres of British life – was entertaining the possibility of leaving the country if a particular Labour leader entered 10 Downing Street as prime minister. All of this ultimately resulted in the EHRC finding the party responsible for three breaches of the 2010 Equality Act (passed by a Labour government): political interference in anti-Semitism complaints, failure to provide adequate training to those handling anti-Semitism complaints, and harassment. Labour's proud anti-discrimination traditions were dragged through the mud under the destructive Corbyn experiment.

Corbyn may have gone, but the party's indulgence of ugly racialised politics continues to be a bit of a problem. New leader Sir Keir Starmer did not start off on the strongest footing, making some very questionable shadow-cabinet choices – such as appointing as shadow justice secretary David Lammy (now shadow foreign secretary), a politician who personifies the journey of the Labour Party from a mature and inclusive political party to an amateurish and divisive identitarian outfit. Lammy, who has served as MP for Tottenham since 2000, was once a serious politician who showed great courage in taking on sensitive issues. Indeed, in my early adulthood he was one of the politicians I admired most. His was a sound voice during the London riots a decade ago. He emphasised the destructive effects of long-term worklessness. He stressed that meaningful employment provides a sense of self-worth and structure, and lies at the heart of responsible fatherhood in working-class communities. In the early 2010s Lammy spoke a great deal about fatherlessness and the lack of responsible male role models in the communities he knew. He feared that this was fuelling knife crime in London. Back then, he managed to blend a strong commitment to social justice with an honest, family-oriented traditionalism. But though he was once a mature champion of an inclusive multiracial democracy, he has now established himself as one of the most divisive high-profile figures in our race-relations debate.

Lammy has been responsible for peddling conspiracy theories over the Grenfell Tower fire, claiming that the official death toll was 'far too low' and that the authorities may have deliberately under-reported the number as part of an alleged cover-up – something for which he had no evidence.[17] He also attacked Sir Martin Moore-Bick, the retired Court of Appeal judge appointed to lead the Grenfell Inquiry, arguing that a 'white, upper-middle-class man' should not have been placed in such a role.[18] There is no doubt that the Harvard-educated Lammy appears – on paper – well suited to the role of shadow justice secretary. In this sense, Starmer's appointment of him in a shadow-cabinet role is understandable. But to peddle racial identity politics in such an opportunistic manner over the Grenfell Tower blaze demonstrates a fundamental lack of judgement – it is inflammatory and divisive.

More recently, Lammy hit the headlines for bemoaning the lack of a 'Black English' option for census respondents when asked about their ethnicity. His complaint was that you are allowed to choose 'White English' as your ethnic group, so why not 'Black English'?[19] English identity is not racially exclusive. In fact, the vast majority of English people think that being English has nothing to do with skin colour – it is more about support for communitarian values, appreciating England's cultural heritage and having an understanding of the nation's rich history. Besides, black respondents to the census who wish to express their Englishness can simply choose 'English' as their national identity and 'Black' as their ethnicity. The census does not deny anyone their right to be both black and English – the options are readily available for individuals to report their 'Black English' self-identification. Lammy was clearly guilty of being an identitarian opportunist. We do need more politicians and public figures to speak up for an inclusive, post-racial Englishness, but the likes of Lammy are not well positioned to be the messengers for this project.

But Lammy is far from alone in being a Labour politician making provocative comments about racial and religious minorities. Following the release in March 2021 of a report from the Commission on Race and Ethnic Disparities (CRED) that concluded that factors such as family dynamics and community culture have a greater impact on life chances than race alone, Labour MP Clive Lewis tweeted a picture of a Ku Klux Klan member with the caption 'Move along. Nothing to see here #RaceReport'.[20] You would struggle to find a finer example of the left-wing tendency to label anyone who takes a different view on these matters a bigot. Lewis is certainly no stranger to indulging in divisive identity politics. According to a leaked internal strategy presentation in February 2021, it was advised that Labour must make 'use of the [Union] flag, veterans [and] dressing smartly' as part of a radical rebranding project designed to rebuild trust with disillusioned voters.[21] Unsurprisingly, the progressive-activist wing of the party responded in hysterical fashion. Lewis, the master of poor takes, decried the move as a form of 'Fatherland-ism' and argued that there was a better way to 'build social cohesion than moving down the track of the nativist right'.[22] According to Lewis, taking pride in the Union flag, respecting those who have served in the armed forces and being smartly dressed are pandering to extreme right-wing xenophobia. The patriotic and respectful sentiments that run deep in many British ethnic-minority communities will be fleshed out in greater detail in Chapter 5.

Then there was a comment in Parliament from Labour's Dawn Butler. Addressing rising Tory star Kemi Badenoch (a regular target of activist opprobrium), the Brent Central MP referred to the authors of the CRED report as 'racial gatekeepers'.[23] For those unfamiliar with the term, 'racial gatekeeper' refers to the idea that some non-white individuals adopt conservative policy positions in order to be 'embraced' by their white peers. (Butler herself offered this explanation in a tweet after the debate.) Equally worrying was that, in a recent Commons debate, Butler had cited work from Dr Shola Mos-Shogbamimu and Professor Kehinde Andrews, two of the most toxic contributors to the race-relations debate. Mos-Shogbamimu called Dr Tony Sewell – lead author of the CRED report – a 'token Black man'.[24] Meanwhile, Andrews once referred to Sir Trevor Phillips, the former head of the EHRC, as the embodiment of the 'modern day Uncle Tom'.[25]

The CRED report was published after the BLM protests held in response to the police killing of George Floyd in the US state of Minnesota. In this context, it was inevitable that a report that challenged tired and simplistic orthodoxies about racial identity and its influence on life chances would be received with much scepticism by the contemporary British left. But Labour's problem was that it bent over backwards to please party activists who took an uncritical view of the BLM movement (and the affiliate political organisation BLM UK).

A mature British social-democratic party would have kept a safe distance from a US-centric socio-political movement that has been associated with radical objectives such as the dismantling of the market economy and the defunding of police forces, and that has a history of supporting direct action. While there is work to do in Britain to strengthen equality of opportunity and repair institutional trust, socio-economic disparities are all too often simplistically framed as direct products of 'systemic racism'. Labour's identitarian left refuses to entertain the influence of other factors, such as family structure and community dynamics, which can also feed into racial and ethnic disparities. These identitarians have little helpful to contribute to debates on social progress.

But the Labour Party's identitarian woes never seem to end. One of its most notorious pro-Corbyn politicians from the 2019 intake – Leicester East MP Claudia Webbe – was found guilty of harassment in October 2021 after making threatening phone calls to a woman who was having an affair with her partner, which allegedly included a threat to use acid against her. She had already had the Labour whip withdrawn, pending the outcome of the trial, but she still received glowing character references from one-time comrades, such as former Labour leader Jeremy Corbyn and former shadow home secretary Diane Abbott. But district judge Paul Goldspring said he found Webbe to be 'vague, incoherent and at times illogical' – ultimately finding her to be 'untruthful'.[26]

Webbe's guilty verdict provides a further indictment of the Corbyn era. Webbe had spent much of her political career as a London borough councillor in Corbyn's constituency of Islington. For the 2019 general election, she was controversially chosen – by Labour's NEC, of which she was a member – as Labour's candidate for Leicester East, ahead of long-serving local Labour councillors. Her selection prompted accusations that Labour was parachuting Corbyn allies into safe seats. Following Webbe's selection, Labour's party chair for Leicester East at the time, John Thomas, resigned his party membership. He called her selection a 'fix and a disgrace'.[27]

Webbe's candidature showcased the toxic mix of racial identity politics and political cynicism at the heart of the Corbyn project. Her selection was primarily justified on the grounds of her race and sex, rather than her track record as a public servant – or, indeed, her competence or intelligence. It was clear as day that voters were not impressed. As Labour crashed to a devastating defeat in December 2019, its vote share in Leicester East dropped by 16 percentage points – with the Tory share of the vote increasing by 14 percentage points. Labour's majority was slashed from 22,428 to 6,019 votes. Furthermore, having been parachuted into the constituency, Webbe was clueless about local concerns. Her vocal opposition to India's territorial claims on the disputed region of Kashmir was particularly unpopular with the area's many voters of Indian Hindu origin. Her selection even prompted Sundip Meghani, an ex-Labour Leicester City councillor, to accuse the party of harbouring anti-Indian sentiments and to resign his party membership.[28]

As a politician Webbe has hardly covered herself in glory. She was simultaneously the MP for Leicester East and the councillor for Bunhill ward in Islington, but breached Parliament's code of conduct by failing to declare ongoing payments from Islington Council for more than half a year.[29] Furthermore, instead of taking responsibility for her actions, she has all too often claimed racial discrimination in a pathetic attempt to deflect criticism. For example, after I suggested on Twitter that 'serving' both as an MP in the East Midlands and as an Islington Borough councillor in north London was not an acceptable arrangement for a public servant, Ms Webbe proceeded to accuse me of 'anti-black hate'. After the guilty verdict, she has faced calls for her to resign as an MP. That would certainly be the decent thing to do, but it is unlikely to happen. Much of the blame for her rise can be laid at the door of Labour's Corbyn experiment – a disastrous political project mired in racial identity politics and cronyism, enabled by 'soft-left' moderates who showed a lack of spine in challenging it from within. And our democracy is all the poorer for it.

In my view, there are three problems which underpin Labour's identity-politics crisis: its historical association with unaccountable identitarian organisations which are not representative of British Muslim communities, its inability to think critically about 'anti-racism' movements which originate in different countries, and a deep-rooted cultural obsession with racial and ethnic representation which has given rise to sheer mediocrity within its internal party structures. In a sense, Labour's fraternisation with certain religio-political organisations and radical trans zealots is completely out of sync with the majority of British Muslims, who are anti-Islamist social traditionalists who are worried about both the threat of Islamist extremism and the impact of identitarian moral degeneracy. The values conflict between ethnic-minority social conservatives and radical cultural liberals on the British left will be discussed in more detail in Chapter 4.

We may be in the post-Corbyn and post-BLM era, but racial identity politics continues to be a problem for the Labour Party. Of course, it may not matter for the next general election – which is likely to be dominated by the devastating socio-economic impacts of the cost-of-living crisis. But the worry is that Labour tends to 'racialise' any crisis under the sun – and the pledge to introduce a new Race Equality Act in one of the leading industrialised nations in the world is a classic example of how left-wing identitarianism has infected Labour's policy-making processes. The party cannot allow itself to be seduced by controversial social movements and divisive political organisations which prioritise identity-driven interests over broad-based cohesion, as it only serves to undermine the party's electoral credibility in the mainstream. It is one thing to think that Britain needs to bolster racial fairness and equality of opportunity – but it is quite another to believe that it is a fundamentally racist society where opportunities for minorities are severely restricted. I would personally argue that Britain provides ample opportunities for traditional family-oriented ethnic minorities to progress and thrive – the 'system' is not deliberately rigged against them.

And we cannot ignore the fact that Labour – while ranking highly in terms of 'diversity' and 'representation' – suffers from a worrying dearth of thoughtful, intellectual ethnic-minority politicians. All too often, its politicians from racial minorities have played the 'race card' when criticised over their woeful political takes, inflammatory comments and outrageous behaviour. In fact, some of them have proven to be political liabilities who continually embarrass the party in the public domain – especially on matters of race and cohesion. Take, for example, Labour's former shadow minister for community cohesion, Bradford West MP Naz Shah, who once remarked that Prevent – the government-led, multi-agency programme that exists to safeguard individuals and communities from the threat of terrorism – had alienated the 'British Muslim community'.[30] Yet a March 2020 study published by crime-and-justice consultancy Crest Advisory found that over half – 56 per cent – of British Muslims had never even heard of Prevent.[31] It would be worth asking Ms Shah how one could be alienated from a government-run scheme that one was unaware of. For that matter, she should also be taken to task over using the homogenising phrase 'British Muslim community' – a mythical concept that masks the various theological and socio-political fractures within the UK's Muslim population.

I suspect I am not alone in holding the view that British democracy is crying out for a sensible left-of-centre party that blends social-justice commitments with a family-oriented traditionalism. Labour's priority should be to develop practical policies which help families maintain a decent standard of living. Labour-market security, family-friendly tax policies and targeted welfare support for the most vulnerable should be high on the list. Of course, the contemporary British left should absolutely be in the business of calling out those who discriminate on the grounds of protected characteristics such as race, ethnicity, religion or sexual orientation (as enshrined in the Labour-passed 2010 Equality Act). But it should refrain from overindulging in the American-inspired politics of intersectionality – fragmenting the working classes in the way the party did before the 2019 general election is the politics of division and defeat.

Fighting discrimination on the grounds of identity is not the same as believing that 'protected characteristics' are the primary factors which feed into various forms of social and economic disadvantage in modern Britain. Labour's response to the CRED report – a landmark piece of research – was anything but mature and considered. As well as the racially motivated abuse hurled at the report's authors by a number of MPs, the party's BLM-inspired response exposed both the intellectual deficit and moral courage at the heart of the party's thinking.

Labour's identity-politics problem is classic 'comfort-zone' politics – peddling the belief that underwhelming ethnic-minority outcomes must be down to 'structural disadvantage' and 'systemic racism'. In these political circles, there is no meaningful discussion to be had on family structure, cultural values cultivated in the household or societal dynamics within particular communities. These factors may well be viewed as inconveniences – but they are influential determinants of life chances in their own right, and their existence means that using racism as a 'catch-all' explanation won't wash with most of the British public, including a substantial proportion of ethnic-minority communities. The depressing reality is that an unpleasant mixture of American-inspired left-wing identitarianism and politically correct social liberalism has led to the problem of family breakdown being left by the wayside when Labour politicians discuss disparities and inequalities in modern Britain. That must change.

3

IN DEFENCE OF THE FAMILY

When I consider the growing disconnect between the modern British left and traditional ethnic minorities, my mind immediately thinks of 'the family'. For many traditional ethnic-minority voters, the immediate family is not only their primary source of social support – it is what they live for. A considerable part of serving their faith is respecting the duties and responsibilities towards family members. Family elders – especially grandparents – are usually treated as enlightened sources of knowledge and wisdom: much-adored individuals who are to be treasured. In my experience of living in Luton, I can safely say that, more times than not, localised multigenerational family networks can be an incredible source of belonging and rootedness – especially for the young. This is precisely why I feel for younger, aspirational, family-oriented Londoners who are being 'pressured out' of their own local communities – especially those who would love to buy a home and raise a family near their elders, but who are being priced out by the capital's largely dysfunctional housing market.

Rates of family breakdown and intergenerational disconnection are notably higher among the white-British majority when compared with a number of Britain's ethnic minorities. According to 2019 ONS data, around one in five white-British dependent children (up to the age of 15 years) is part of a lone-parent family.[1] To put this in perspective, for Britain's Indian, Bangladeshi and Pakistani ethnic groups, this figure drops to 6, 12 and 14 per cent respectively.[2] Of course, there is a debate to be had about problematic cultural practices within oft-romanticised South Asian families who may appear 'stable' on the surface – especially when it comes to female educational and economic empowerment, and, on the fringes, honour-based abuse in relatively closed-off, residentially segregated communities. But, overall, there is perhaps a need for the white-British mainstream to understand how family structure and culture feed into forms of academic success in Asian-origin communities.

While the identitarian activists of the BLM movement are utterly obsessed with portraying Britain as a country plagued by anti-black institutional racism, they are rather silent over the fact that 63 per cent of dependent children of black-Caribbean heritage belong to lone-parent families.[3] At 43 per cent, the figure is also uncomfortably high among their co-racial peers of African origin.[4] If young black lives truly mattered to social-justice warriors and virtue-signallers in Britain, they would explore the impact of relatively high rates of family breakdown and the 'fatherlessness epidemic' in London's inner-city communities. Does the disintegration of two-parent families and shortage of responsible male role models in the household leave young people – especially young men – searching for 'role models' and a sense of belonging through gang membership? Does gang membership in turn heighten the probability of involvement in unlawful activity? While these are admittedly sensitive questions, they must be asked.

One of the better recent interventions in the space of family policy was a report written by the children's commissioner for England, Dame Rachel de Souza. Among her findings were that half of English children now live across more than one household and a quarter of families are headed by a lone parent (of whom 90 per cent are women).[5] It represented a welcome corrective in a social-policy debate that has far too often emphasised 'protected characteristics' such as race, and downplayed other important forms of social and economic disadvantage. Dame Rachel, who for a long time worked as an educationalist in my home town of Luton, rightly noted that families can have a 'protective effect', shielding people in challenging times as well as having a positive impact on both happiness and future earnings:

Having a stable and supportive family, whatever form that takes, can determine a child's future success. Children with happy families do better in their exams, go on to get better jobs, and have higher hourly income at the age of 25. Family can insulate us from life's adversity and challenges.[6]

This is a drum I have been banging for some time. For too long, the social-policy space has been paralysed by political correctness when it comes to discussing the importance of the traditional family in shaping life chances. There are two key questions in the family debate in Britain: how influential is family structure when it comes to shaping personal development? And which 'family models' are most strongly associated with positive youth outcomes? Prominent think tanks such as the Centre for Social Justice (CSJ) have produced research which highlights the reality that family structure matters. While it may be an inconvenience to those who view the nuclear family unit as a reactionary institution that is a roadblock to social progress, we cannot afford to ignore the close correlation between family structure and various outcomes relating to youth development.

In the words of the CSJ's Sophia Worringer: 'Robust academic research has shown that family structure has a greater impact on the presence of externalising behaviours – linked to cognitive development, physical and mental health, school attainment, criminal-justice involvement and social and emotional development – than education or poverty.'[7] This supports research produced by Rob Henderson of the US-based Institute for Family Studies which suggests that family instability during childhood is more strongly associated with psychopathic behaviours in adulthood than early-life socio-economic status.[8]

Family structure can trump socio-economic resources when it comes to shaping youth outcomes such as academic performance, mental health, physical well-being and cognitive development, yet it continues to be largely overlooked in Britain social-policy debates. For the identitarian left, emphasising the importance of family dynamics undermines their own efforts to place racial identity at the heart of discussions on social and economic disadvantage. Meanwhile, for radical social liberals (and it is worth noting that a fair number of them are in the modern Conservative Party), the mildest defence of the family unit is viewed as a threat to their feminist ideology and somehow amounts to the vilification of single mothers.

Of course, there are single mothers across Britain who do everything in their power to raise their children in a decent and proper way – encouraging them to excel in everything they do and make positive contributions to their local communities. A child belonging to a lone-parent family can go on to achieve great things and live a stable life of peace and prosperity; another child from a two-parent household can go on to be a spectacular underachiever and end up in the criminal-justice system. But this is ultimately a matter of which kind of family structure is *most strongly associated* with positive youth outcomes and the type of household dynamic which is most likely to have a positive impact on young people's personal development.

This was a key point made in the March 2021 CRED report:

> There are many different family structures that can provide a happy childhood, including millions of single parents doing a loving and effective job in difficult circumstances. It is clear, however, that there continues to be a need for more explicit public policy promotion of parental and family support. We reject both the stigmatisation of single mothers and the turning of a blind eye to the impact of family breakdown on the life chances of children.[9]

There has been a cultural revolution of sorts in British family life over the past half a century. This has included more accepting social attitudes towards divorce and greater female empowerment, which has increased human freedom. There are models beyond the conventional nuclear family that are workable. However, alongside these beneficial changes, the prevalence of family breakdown has increased. Of course, we must not ignore the economic stresses on households of our competitive market economy, pressures that can undermine the overall quality of family life. But, equally, mainstream cultural shifts on the importance of marriage as an institution and the recalibrated trade-off between individual freedom and collective responsibility should not be overlooked.

Irrespective of how toxic a marriage becomes, divorce is not necessarily an outcome to be celebrated. Indeed, the fact that 'divorce parties' are now an established form of 'celebration' in modern Britain and other parts of the Western world is itself an indicator of moral decay – especially given that children are all too often entangled in marital breakdown. The notion that holding a party to mark the disintegration of a relationship helps one to salvage one's dignity is bizarre – it is one of the most undignified acts unimaginable and fundamentally disrespectful towards the institution of marriage.

Demonstrating how devastating marital breakdown can be on youth development, a 2022 study published by the journal *Demographic Research* found that divorce had a larger impact than parental death on young people's educational attainment.[10] Based on data drawn from 17 countries, the study shows – quite interestingly – that the negative effect of divorce on educational attainment appears to be stronger for the children of higher-educated parents. Why? The answer could be that these children have more to lose in terms of both financial and non-financial resources. Meanwhile, lower-educated parents traditionally have relatively few 'parental resources' to begin with, meaning the drop-off in resources resulting from divorce is less steep – the so-called 'floor effect'.

In recent times, the number of divorces in Britain has been on an upward trajectory. The ONS have shown that, in England and Wales, there was a total of 111,934 opposite-sex divorces in 2021 – an increase of 9.3 per cent from the 2020 figure. Divorce enquiries to British legal firms soared during the Covid-19 pandemic, with lockdowns and social distancing ending what were previously 'separate' routines and external leisure activities that served to mask underlying marital problems. With family courts suspending operations over the course of the pandemic, Britain could be on the verge of a post-Covid divorce explosion – especially with the liberalising no-fault divorce reforms introduced under the Conservative government.

So there is a debate to be had over what the institution of marriage means to different sections of British society. Have the forces of market individualism reshaped the reality of marriage in Britain today? Individual freedom and personal self-interest can be very much at odds with more traditional understandings of marriage which are ultimately rooted in the value of self-sacrifice and the nurturing of the next generation. While these collectivistic framings of marriage continue to endure in some of Britain's ethnic and religious minorities, they have been steadily eroded in the relatively secularised and atomised mainstream. For decades, that mainstream has consistently undervalued the negative impacts of divorce. The *Demographic Research* study confirms that parental divorce can be an incredibly traumatic experience for children. While it is admittedly sensitive territory, there now needs to be a frank national conversation about the risks of marital breakdown and the degree of public respect for marriage as a social institution with moral obligations.

This is not simply an issue of children being left in lone-parent households following marital breakdown, but also of the risks attached to non-marital romantic arrangements and their potential impact on Britain's young people. Could it be that the problem is not only divorce, but the fact that not as many child-producing couples are getting married to begin with? Traditional think tanks such as the CSJ have certainly stuck their heads above the parapet over this particular dimension of the debate. It has called the 'marriage gap' a social-justice issue. Including both opposite- and same-sex marriages in its analysis, the CSJ has shown that married parents are twice as likely to stay together as cohabiting ones. By the time they turn five years of age, over half – 53 per cent – of children of cohabiting parents will have experienced their parents' separation; among five-year-olds with married parents, this drops to 15 per cent – an astonishing difference of 38 percentage points.[11]

While the institution of marriage continues to be highly prioritised in traditional ethnic-minority communities of faith – especially in those of South Asian origin – it has been eroded in the mainstream. The figures I have looked at in my own research are both striking and concerning. In 1971, the UK had 570,000 single-parent families; by 2021, this figure had reached an eye-watering 3 million.[12] In the 1970s, the marriage rate for men – that is, the number of men marrying per 1,000 unmarried people of either sex aged 16 years and over – peaked at 78.4 in 1974. By 2019, this had plummeted to just 18.6.[13]

For women, the 1970s peak was 60.5 (in 1972). This had dropped to 17.2 by 2019.[14] Of course, it would be silly to deny the existence of toxic marriages that can have a negative impact on the well-being of children – but we must remain hard-headed and be honest about the patterns of association. Marriage, compared to cohabitation, is *more likely* to neutralise the threat of relationship breakdown, and thus is *more strongly linked* with a form of two-parent stability that is *more strongly associated* with positive youth outcomes. In this sense, the broader social benefits of marriage in terms of family stability and young people's personal development should not be downplayed just because some cases go against the grain.

These differences do matter – separations of this nature in a young child's formative years can be detrimental to foundational personal development. Family stability has been shown to affect children's outcomes profoundly. Even when controlling for income and education, children raised in unstable families suffer poorer health and are more likely to be excluded from school, to take on gang membership, or not to be in education, employment or training (NEET). The social and economic cost is correctly acknowledged by Worringer in her CSJ report: 'The cost of this to the NHS, to the criminal justice system, and to the Treasury – in terms of lost revenues – is huge. Less quantifiable but equally corrosive is the impact on society: the anti-social behaviour of even a tiny minority can erode trust and well-being among the majority.'[15]

The growing evidence in the British context points towards this: family stability is integral to young people's personal development, with a two-parent household spearheaded by a married couple being the 'social model' most strongly linked with childhood family-life stability. Once again, this is not to take away from the incredible love and commitment shown by many single parents towards their children growing up in modern Britain. And we should push back on the stigmatisation of single mothers. Single parenthood is a product of one parent (usually the father) abandoning the other (usually the mother) – which means that the moral fault should not lie on the side of the single parent (usually the mother) left to care for the youngest in society. Indeed, perhaps there should be a greater social focus on feckless and commitment-phobic men who have fathered children but have failed to take on the duties and responsibilities that come with being a father. Rather, we should be honest about the family structures most strongly linked to positive youth outcomes in important spheres of life such as health and education. While two parents are not always better than one, it certainly heightens the chances of parental duties – the amount of time, energy, attention and resources required to raise children in a solid and proper manner – being 'spread out' beyond a single individual.

The contemporary British left simply cannot afford to obsess over protected characteristics – such as race and ethnicity – when it comes to developing a social-policy agenda which is fit for purpose. The list of such characteristics – as enshrined in the Equality Act 2010, passed under the New Labour government – is insufficient in terms of providing the foundations for an effective approach to tackling inequalities in Britain. There is no complacency to be tolerated on this front – Britain is a land of profound social breakdown, with both low marriage rates and stubbornly high levels of family disintegration. And the fact that more and more research is being done into worrying levels of loneliness among both the elderly and the young tells a depressing story of intergenerational disconnection. Traditional bonds, whereby the youth looked up to grandparents and community elders, who possess far more life experience and have been through more pain and suffering than many of them could possibly imagine, are being lost – especially in the mainstream.

Whether or not one belongs to a loving and stable family unit remains one of the most influential determinants in the shaping of life chances and personal development – irrespective of racial background, ethnic heritage or religious affiliation. And we should not dismiss the benefits of loving grandparents – who may well have a story or two about taking on life's toughest challenges and various forms of trauma – playing active roles in a young person's development. While the UK fares well internationally when it comes to providing anti-discrimination protections on the grounds of race, ethnicity and religion – certainly better than European countries such as France, Germany and the Netherlands – it has the unfortunate reputation of being a global leader when it comes to family breakdown. Indeed, while it may fare better in terms of race relations and community cohesion than other diverse European democracies, those countries tend to value the family unit and the institution of marriage more highly, as reflected in their government spending commitments and tax system.

It is time to recognise that a stable family unit remains the finest social safety net known to humankind. And we should be unafraid of saying that a two-parent household led by a married couple is the social model most strongly linked with positive youth outcomes relating to school attainment, mental health, physical well-being, cognitive development and law-abiding behaviour. This is not reactionary ideology – it is what the existing research tells us. I was delighted to see Dame Rachel's rallying cry for the family to be at the heart of all key government decisions. The restoration of the family at the centre of social policy is essential in our efforts to foster a more resilient society in the post-Brexit world.

And there is a metric that should be better prioritised in Britain's social-policy space – arguably one of my favourite all-encompassing measures regarding well-being: life satisfaction. An essential part of subjective welfare, it is an assessment of well-being in terms of mood, satisfaction with relationships, achieved goals and self-perceived ability to cope with the challenges of everyday life. In her study 'Family system characteristics, parental behaviors, and adolescent family life satisfaction', Oklahoma State

University professor Carolyn S. Henry concluded that an adolescent's life satisfaction is heavily influenced by their family's cultural dynamics and structural characteristics.[16] The more bonding and support there is within a family, the greater the adolescent's life satisfaction. Results of this study also revealed that adolescents living in a single-parent family home had significantly lower life satisfaction than adolescents in a two-parent home.

Research I have done into the relationship between childhood family life and adult life satisfaction has provided some striking findings. A nationally representative survey of 1,000 British adults, carried out in January 2021, asked respondents to evaluate how (un)stable their family life was during their childhood and to report how (dis)satisfied they were with their current life in Britain. Firstly, it is worth mentioning the intergenerational differences in perceived childhood family stability. While 87 per cent of British respondents aged 55 years and over reported having a stable childhood family life, this dropped to 66 per cent for those aged 18–24 years.[17] While 8 per cent of respondents aged 55 years and over reported having an unstable family life during their childhood, this figure shot up to 28 per cent for respondents aged 18–24 years.[18] There is of course the (remote) possibility that, as people get older, their perceptions of their own childhoods change, but it is unlikely that this would largely explain such significant age-group differences. There may even be generational shifts in what 'family stability' constitutes – expectations can play some part in this. But I suspect that it is far more likely that such survey figures reflect longer-term trends in family breakdown and notable shifts in family structure. However, irrespective of the causes, the fact that nearly three in ten 18-to-24-year-olds in Britain believe they had an unstable family life during their childhood represents both a social and moral failure.

The link between childhood family life and adult life satisfaction cannot be ignored by social-policy specialists who genuinely care about the well-being of Britain. In the British adult population, 47 per cent of people who reported having a *stable* childhood family life stated they were satisfied with their own life in the present day. The figure for current life satisfaction dropped to only 26 per cent for people who said that they had an *unstable* family life during their childhood.[19] In the subset of British respondents who reported having a stable childhood family life, slightly more than one in four – 26 per cent – said they were dissatisfied with their own life, compared to 49 per cent of those who reported having an unstable family life during their childhood. Crucially, in an advanced statistical model controlling for a string of socio-demographic characteristics – such as age, gender, ethnicity, education level and social class – reporting a stable childhood family life was significantly associated with a higher likelihood of reporting adult life satisfaction.[20]

The modern British left is failing by refusing to acknowledge the value of stable family structures to young people's personal development and wider life satisfaction.

It should celebrate the social value of robust family structures which characterise many of Britain's ethnic-minority communities – such as the high-flying and aspirational Chinese-heritage families of Longsight in Manchester or the Indian-origin households of Osterley in west London. These are not 'white-adjacent' families sustaining the structures of 'racial supremacy'; rather, they are traditional, family-oriented people who wish to live in peace and prosperity. This is to be admired, not vilified. For instance, despite being relatively deprived as an ethnic group, young British Bangladeshis – who are notably less likely to live in a lone-parent household than those in the mainstream – are lifting education levels in their own communities. When examining impressive British Bangladeshi educational attainment, notable improvements at a select number of schools in London's eastern boroughs – particularly Newham and Tower Hamlets – should not be overlooked. But it is largely a story of family dynamics, involving first-generation-migrant parents who may not be formally educated themselves but wish for their children to grasp the opportunities provided by English state-funded education, and thereby to overcome relative material deprivation.

Contemporary liberal-leftists in Britain are not doing traditional ethnic minorities any favours by obsessing over protected characteristics – such as race, ethnicity, religious belief, sexual orientation and gender assignment – when looking to set the 'equality' narrative. Many in those communities are fully aware that all is not well in the

British social mainstream – one plagued by relatively high rates of family breakdown and intergenerational disconnection. Parental support and intergenerational bonds must be part of the discussion on how to bolster young people's development in modern Britain. While there is a debate to be had on the level of state support needed by communities most at risk of family break-down, the CRED report was correct to say that 'the support, nurture and care that family networks provide are something that no government intervention can match in practical or emotional power'.[21] I suspect that this is a statement – extracted from a report that a group of UN 'experts' absurdly concluded was guilty of normal-ising 'white supremacy' – that would be met with much agreement in traditional, non-white, ethnic-minority communities across Britain.

The contemporary British left is not only guilty of importing foreign-inspired racial identity politics – it has also entertained unapologetically anti-family agendas manufactured in radical American faculties that have a fundamental hatred of traditional social institutions, which they consider 'hierarchical' and 'reactionary'. This is not necessarily a new phenomenon in the field of academia. Take, for example, the deceased Canadian American rad-ical feminist and writer Shulamith Firestone. Born in 1945, she was a central figure in the early development of second-wave feminism, notorious for having, in January 1968, organised a mock 'funeral' at Arlington National Cemetery marking the 'burial of traditional womanhood'.

One of her most famous quotes is all too often recited by today's anti-family activists: 'the family structure is the source of psychological, economic and political oppression.'[22] After her struggles with mental illness and reportedly self-induced starvation, Firestone was found dead in her New York apartment in 2012 at the age of 67. Her landlord suspected that Firestone had been dead for a week before she was discovered (after neighbours had smelt an odour coming from her flat).

Firestone was no doubt an influential academic, writer and activist – but I am not sure that she is the type of figure that the modern British left should draw inspiration from. Labour's grossly immature 'abolish the family' activists should not be given the time of day by the party leadership. Sir Keir Starmer may bore some in his party by continually referring to his 'toolmaker' father and his mother who worked as an NHS nurse, and to the values of hard work and compassion they instilled in him, but it certainly doesn't make me switch off. In fact, Starmer could be a leading force when it comes to the rejuvenation of family-friendly, pro-marriage politics on the left – he has the personal life story to back it up. Married to Victoria Alexander since 2007 – his only marriage – he has two young children, a son and a daughter, both born in wedlock, who are being raised in their mother's Jewish faith. It certainly makes quite the contrast from the profile of a certain recent Conservative prime minister.

There are far too many middle-class liberal-leftists who refuse to embrace the reality that stable, two-parent families produce the best outcomes – even though they themselves tend to be married and their own families generally match this description. Indeed, plenty of them were raised by married couples in well-structured, two-parent homes. Therein lies the paradox: many of our liberal-left politicians are not keen on promoting any kind of social conservatism despite living rather socially conservative lives themselves. It is rank hypocrisy of the highest order to express approval of lifestyle choices that you would never make for yourself – especially when you are an elected representative who should be interested in the general betterment of society. Instead of desperately hoping to come across as 'fashionable' by going with the latest socio-cultural trends, liberal-left politicians – especially those with rather traditional and stable family histories – should summon the courage to hammer home this very point: progressivism needs conservatism. If the left truly cares about social progress and young people's advancement, then it needs to do more to promote family-friendly thinking in the social-policy realm.

Indeed, there is a social-democratic defence of the family that can be offered – one that takes aim at capitalistic mindsets. Market-driven individualism – with its emphasis on naked self-interest and encouragement of personal greed – can pose a threat to family stability and social solidarity, alienating family-oriented ethnic and religious minorities who are anxious about perceived trends towards cultural decadence and moral decay. Furthermore, the widening disconnect between the modern British left and traditional religious minorities means that there was an opening for the centre right to show its appreciation for collectivistic cultures which emphasise family unity, civic duty and social rootedness. This, of course, would have required 'conservatives' to confront some uncomfortable truths. As it stands, though, the Tories are simply incapable of doing so – with far too many adopting a largely uncritical view of market forces and failing to offer a compelling traditionalist defence of the family unit and the institution of marriage.

Of course, the modern British left should guard against the romanticisation of the family unit, and it should challenge how cultural and religious values are used within some ethnic-minority families to severely restrict the educational growth and financial status of female members – wives, daughters, sisters, cousins, nieces, as well as younger-generation in-laws. It should be in the business of standing up for and protecting the most vulnerable in society – meaning that it ought to adopt a tough law-and-order approach to domestic abuse in families that live in closed and segregated communities on the fringes of society. This is the bread-and-butter feminism which has been neglected on the left due to political correctness and identitarian sensitivities.

The left can do this, and ultimately adopt the general view that the conventional two-parent family unit, the institution of marriage and the decades-gathered wisdom of grandparents can be powerful agents of youth development in our country. Competing against a Conservative

Party which has far too many politicians who obsess over low taxes and light-touch regulation, there is an electoral market for a social-democratic traditionalism that views a variety of public policy areas – housing, healthcare, education, employment, childcare, crime – through a family-oriented lens. In the middle of the country's cost-of-living woes – where affordable family-friendly homes and well-paid secure jobs are relatively scarce – an inclusive political force characterised by 'social-justice traditionalism' could gather considerable public support. And while we are all in favour of lifting schooling standards and the quality of teaching, there has to be an understanding that educational progress is better facilitated through active parental interest and involvement. As the head of the CSJ's family research unit, Cristina Odone, recently remarked: family, far more than school, shapes children's outcomes.[23]

If the modern British left genuinely wants to shore up and consolidate its ethnic-minority support – as well as win back traditional and aspirational non-white voters who have distanced themselves from the left in recent times – then it must place the family at the heart of both its policy-creating and narrative-setting activities. But there is another, closely related problem that it must address. The Labour Party is often referred to as a 'broad church' – but a radical, secular liberalism threatens to take over the contemporary British left. Cultural modernists who sneer at the slightest mention of God, devotion to faith and religious belief are no friends of Britain's traditional ethnic minorities. Indeed, there is an overlap: those who undermine the importance of family also tend to underappreciate the immense social value of faith in modern Britain.

4

THE POWER OF FAITH

It is a question that has sparked some of the most intensely contested debates in modern times: are faith and religion a force for good in the world?

I am often left wondering whether the decline of faith and religious devotion has served Britain well. There is no doubt that much evil is done in the world in the name of religion. On the grounds of 'defending' and 'protecting' their faith, terrorists all over the world have killed, maimed and tortured. Looking to assert their dominance in their respective nation states, militant fundamentalists itch to curtail the rights of religious minorities. Radical ideologues relish peddling narratives of 'group superiority' over those of different religious affiliations. It is no surprise that robust secularist thought and a general public scepticism of religion's value have developed in the UK. A series of devastating, Islamist-inspired terrorist attacks – including the 7/7 London and May 2017 Manchester

Arena suicide bombings – have only served to accelerate this process in the social mainstream. At the latter, which occurred at the end of an Ariana Grande concert, the youngest victim was eight-year-old Saffie-Rose Roussos. According to the 2022 Global Terrorism Index, the primary global terror threat comes in the form of religiously motivated extremism – hardly a glowing endorsement for the 'power of faith'.[1]

The overall decline of religious faith in the UK – driven by the consistently downward trajectory in the level of Anglican devotion in recent decades – has not led to a fundamental breakdown in public order. Most British people continue with their everyday lives in relative peace and prosperity when compared with the rest of the world. On the surface, it does not seem to have done Britain much harm – and ardent secularists may well say, 'We can do without religion.' And, quite frankly, who could blame them for saying this after the disorder in Leicester in August–September 2022, during which eastern parts of the city descended into an Islamist–Hindutva battleground, with dozens of arrests made? Leicester, a Labour-voting city that was traditionally heralded as a paragon of multiculturalism, exposed how delicate social cohesion can be in seemingly peaceable communities across religiously diverse Britain.

This spate of communal violence raised much concern over the degree to which subcontinental-style sectarianism has gained a foothold in our cities – after all, out-of-town troublemakers from London and Birmingham had entered Leicester to exacerbate community tensions. With Leicestershire Police's chief constable Rob Nixon and experienced investigative journalist Sunny Hundal pointing to the disconnection between traditional faith-based leadership and younger disillusioned sections of the migrant-origin population, the Leicester disorders revealed how ultra-religious identity politics – spear-headed by self-absorbed social-media 'clout-chasers' – can take advantage of a lack of spiritual belonging and ineffectual community 'leadership'. To make matters worse, law-and-order responsibilities have all too often been outsourced to such 'faith leaders' – who may not even have social cohesion truly at heart.

Being a British man of Bangladeshi Muslim origin with an academic background in community cohesion and counter-extremism, I fully acknowledge the threat posed to social solidarity by religious extremists and radical ideologues who sow the seeds of division in our liberal-democratic society. This was exposed during the Covid-19 pandemic, with religious ideologues both at home and abroad peddling anti-establishment conspiracy theories and blaming other groups for the spread of the disease. But it is worth injecting a degree of balance into the debate on the value of faith in modern Britain. The Covid-19 pandemic was extremely challenging for many families and communities across the country. We ought to recognise the reality that faith can bolster much-needed forms of determination and resilience when presented with testing circumstances. In times of seemingly never-ending difficulty, it can provide a sense of optimism – a hope that better times are around the corner and the belief that perseverance will reap rewards to be enjoyed in the future.

Belonging to the old-fashioned traditionalist left, I believe that faith can provide an individual with a positive sense of purpose and form the basis for healthy community interactions. Many of Britain's traditional migrant communities are deeply family-oriented, community-spirited and intergenerationally cohesive. Civic associations within such communities continue to flourish, with places of worship providing a spiritually uplifting sense of belonging. The sense of connection one feels by belonging to welcoming faith-based institutions that can be an organic source of social support should be appreciated. This is especially so in an era increasingly defined by social isolation and intergenerational disconnection, which are bound to have longer-term negative impacts on well-being and life satisfaction.

Stable family structures, shared civic institutions and religio-cultural traditions – meaningful sources of advantage that can have a positive impact on young people's development – have been eroded in much of the mainstream while being hallmarks of thriving ethnic-minority communities across Britain. The differences between the white mainstream and non-white minorities are striking when it comes to religiosity and self-declared affiliation. A January 2021 ICM Unlimited survey found that while 34 per cent of white people in the UK felt that their religious identity was important to them, this rose to 63 per cent for their non-white counterparts.[2] While 52 per cent of whites stated that they belonged to a particular religion, this increased to 75 per cent for non-whites.[3] A Savanta ComRes survey in the build-up to the 2019 general election found that 87 per cent of British Muslim respondents (the overwhelming majority belonging to an ethnic-minority group) felt that their religious identity was important to them. Over half of the British Muslims surveyed – 51 per cent – reported that they attended a place of worship for religious services at least once a week.[4]

Many traditional, Labour-voting ethnic-minority communities – among whom faith and religious devotion remain cornerstones of everyday life – are increasingly being left behind by a modern British left dominated by godless, pseudo-revolutionary, 'class-warrior' activists. On top of that, a secular liberalism which is not remotely appreciative of the value of faith and religiously inspired optimism has been mainstreamed – a strand of thinking which overlooks the communitarianism that exists among many Labour-leaning voters with an ethnic-minority background. While it may be an inconvenient truth for atheistic leftists who sneer at those of faith and consider religion to be an obstructor of social advancement, the Labour Party is an institution with a rich Christian social-democratic tradition – and many traditionally left-voting, ethnic-minority communities (spanning a range of religious affiliations) would welcome its revival.

In a market-based society obsessed with macro-economic metrics such as gross domestic product (GDP), important 'human' measures such as life satisfaction are left by the wayside. How contented are our fellow citizens with their own lives? What drives life satisfaction in the society we all live in? Holding a robust religious identity has its advantages – it should not be automatically viewed as a socially undesirable trait.

My own research, based on the January 2021 nationally representative polling by ICM Unlimited referred to above, found a strong link between the personal importance of religious identity and life satisfaction. The survey revealed that 42 per cent of British adults were satisfied with their own lives, with three in ten being dissatisfied. For those who reported that their religious identity was 'very important' to them, the figure for life satisfaction rose to 58 per cent – nearly six in ten people. For those who said that their religious identity was 'not important at all' to them, this figure plummeted to just 30 per cent. For the subset that said their religious identity was very important to them, fewer than one in four reported being dissatisfied with their own life. This jumped to more than 40 per cent for those who said that their religious identity was not important to them at all. While 37 per cent of Britons with no religion said they were satisfied with their own lives, this increased by ten percentage points to 47 per cent for those with a religious affiliation. And while 34 per cent of Brits with no declared religious affiliation reported being dissatisfied with their own life, this dropped to 26 per cent for those with a religious affiliation.[5]

It is worth noting that in advanced statistical models that control for a range of socio-demographic characteristics (such as gender, age, ethnicity, educational level and social class), strength of personal religious identity is significantly positively associated with self-reported life satisfaction.[6] This is very much in keeping with previous research which shows that individuals who value religion and cultural traditions highly tend to report higher rates of life satisfaction. It is commonly accepted around much of the world that religion and spirituality are among some of the most important factors when it comes to mental and physical well-being – providing structure and meaning to behaviour, value systems and life experiences. Researchers at the Minnesota-based Mayo Clinic, a non-profit academic medical centre specialising in integrated healthcare, concluded that most relevant studies 'have shown that religious involvement and spirituality are associated with better health outcomes, including greater longevity, coping skills, and health-related quality of life (even during terminal illness) and less anxiety, depression and suicide'.[7] Indeed, given how much we are learning about the impact of social–emotional aspects of life on general health, religious beliefs and faith-related activities should be an area of considerable focus for the medical research community.

Robin Dunbar, emeritus professor in evolutionary psychology at the University of Oxford, has identified two main explanations for the enduring popularity and attractiveness of religion in an age of more highly educated populations and scientific advancement. The first is that, on average, religious people are generally happier, healthier and live longer, as well as having 'easier deaths' when the time comes. The other is that religious people are more likely to feel that they belong to a community. Dunbar's personal research found that those who attended religious services were depressed less frequently, felt their lives were more worthwhile, were better engaged with their local community and felt a greater level of trust towards others.[8] This is supported by studies, such as Markus Jokela's November 2021 paper for the *American Journal of Epidemiology*, which have concluded that religious attendance is related to lower psychological distress and higher well-being.[9] But one of the wider social benefits of faith is the impact it can have on family stability. In their 2016 book *Soul Mates*, Brad Wilcox and Nicholas Wolfinger found that participation in organised religion increases the likelihood of stable married relationships (which, as discussed in the previous chapter, are incredibly beneficial for young people's well-being and personal development).[10]

The left cannot be in the business of talking about family stability and community spirit without acknowledging the positive impact of faith, religious involvement and spiritual activity. Considering the volume of studies which show the benefits of these things for health-related outcomes such as psychological well-being, the debate about addressing the many social ills that exist in modern Britain needs to take on a different dimension. It should include conversations on belief systems and community structures that provide an individual with a sense of meaning and purpose: religiously inspired forms of resilience, hope and optimism that enable one to withstand and take on the more difficult challenges in life.

This may go down like a lead balloon with vocal public atheists who believe that the left should dismiss religions as unscientific mythical relics; it may also sit uncomfortably with secular rationalists who believe that faith does more harm than good in society. But it would be most refreshing for Britain's traditional, patriotic and law-abiding ethnic minorities – migrant-origin families who have a zero-tolerance approach to religious extremism and sectarian disorder, but believe that a positive and healthy relationship with one's faith can play an integral part in having a stable, peaceful and fulfilling life. This is where Britain needs a mature left that understands the threat of religious identity politics but also appreciates how a shared, inclusive appreciation of faith can provide a sense of connection, rootedness and belonging.

All of this gives rise to the all-important question: why are large parts of the contemporary British left squeamish about embracing a deeper recognition of the value of faith that goes beyond superficial religious identity politics? It appears that Labour is more than happy to entertain unrepresentative Muslim organisations that operate in the industry of grievance and victimhood – with many of its own political amateurs opportunistically accusing others of 'Islamophobia' for raising perfectly legitimate points about multiculturalism and integration. Paralysed by identity politics and political correctness, Labour struggles to talk about what many British Muslims are able to say: that Islamist extremism is the principal terror threat in modern Britain. The 'compassionate' left revels in 'protecting' ethnic-minority Muslims, who are ultimately viewed as 'oppressed others' who have borne the brunt of aggressive post-9/11 securitisation and have seen fellow members of the Ummah – the global Islamic community – suffer in the Middle East for decades at the hands of Western foreign policy. The reality, as I discuss in Chapter 6, is rather different: levels of democratic satisfaction and institutional trust suggest that Britain's ethnic-minority Muslims are anything but a victimised and ostracised monolith that needs to be mollycoddled by the hyper-paternalistic identitarian left. What they could do with is a social-democratic party that respects their decent, traditional values, which are under threat from secular liberal-leftists who are anything but pro-family and have little appreciation for the good that faith and spirituality bring to our society.

Living in a traditionally Labour-voting town with a notable Muslim population, I cannot help but feel that the coalition between ethnic-minority provincial traditionalists and radical metropolitan social liberals is on increasingly shaky ground. There is no doubt in my mind that Labour's continued woke posturing has the potential to alienate many British Muslims who have historically provided the party with steadfast electoral support – from towns such as Luton, Slough, Oldham, Rochdale and Blackburn to the inner-city areas of London, Birmingham, Bradford, Manchester, Leicester and Peterborough.

A recent case study which suggests that a centre-left traditionalist rival could make headway with historically Labour-voting British Muslims is the July 2021 Batley and Spen by-election. The jubilation with which the Labour Party greeted its narrow win was – at the time – a sign of how dreadfully it has performed electorally in by-elections under Sir Keir Starmer's leadership. This includes being soundly beaten by the Tories in Hartlepool in May 2021 and winning a paltry 1.6 per cent of the vote in the Chesham and Amersham by-election just a few weeks later. Labour's majority in the West Yorkshire seat – which it had held since Tony Blair's 1997 general election victory – dropped from 3,525 in 2019 to just 323. On top of that, a rival left-wing candidate, in the form of Workers Party of Britain (WPB) leader George Galloway, collected an impressive vote share of 22 per cent, while Labour's dropped from 43 to 35 per cent.

Labour may rightly feel relieved at holding on to a Leave-voting seat in northern England. But its overzealous celebrations looked more than a little ridiculous – and there is no room for complacency on this front. The Batley by-election signalled the reality that Labour finds itself at the very heart of the British left's own culture war – irrespective of what the polls may tell us and how disastrously the Tories govern the country. After years of appeasing various interest groups with diametrically opposed ideological beliefs and political objectives, Labour is being pulled in all kinds of directions – and it is bursting at the seams. It is highly likely that George Galloway performed particularly well with British Muslim voters in Batley – a reflection of the reality that Labour cannot be both the political arm of Stonewall and the natural party of British Muslim traditionalists. I may be a cynic, but there is not much potential for reconciling radical transgender activism with conventional Islamic teachings. As British Muslim awareness of Labour's social liberalism on issues such as gender self-identification, sexual-minority rights and LGBT relationship teaching grows, support for the party among Britain's sizeable Pakistani and Bangladeshi Sunni Muslim communities may well decline, especially if other economically left-leaning parties take robustly conservative positions on such matters.

As suggested above, Labour is not helped by the many contradictions it now champions in the culture wars. Leading politicians expressing their blind support for gender self-identification on the LGBT website PinkNews may go down an absolute storm among chattering-class Guardianistas, but will likely come a cropper in Labour-voting communities containing ethnic-minority traditionalists who believe in conventional understandings of manhood and womanhood. And its tentative support for policy proposals such as on-demand abortion for any reason up to birth is unlikely to command much backing within Britain's Pakistani- and Bangladeshi-heritage Sunni Muslim communities.

Of course, the likes of Zarah Sultana, a glorified student activist and current Labour MP for Coventry South, try to portray British Muslim communities as bastions of radical progressivism. But I suspect they know this is nonsense – some of the most socially conservative attitudes in Britain are contained in its traditional-minded Muslim communities, which have remained staunchly Labour over decades. The truth is, Labour has simply taken loyal British Muslim voters for granted over many years. Thanks to the LGBT lobby in its midst, Labour finds itself estranging these long-neglected supporters – including many who would consider themselves economically left-wing. One of the greatest 'culture wars' to be fought on the left may be between younger, culturally liberal voters and socially conservative Muslims who traditionally vote Labour.

This, of course, presents an opportunity for a left-wing but traditionalist political alternative – like Galloway's WPB. It could be socially traditional in a domestic sense; adopt foreign-policy positions in line with mainstream British Muslim opinion; be family-oriented and communitarian; criticise the 'LGBT overreach' in our political and social institutions; and highlight forms of anti-Muslim discrimination in, say, the labour market or the private rented-housing sector. Due to the residential distribution of British Muslim voters, a well-organised political outfit along these lines could make life very difficult for Labour in a string of inner-city constituencies and post-industrial towns. Galloway's performance in Batley and Spen should be seen as a warning shot to the Labour Party leadership – it can no longer take the votes of historically Labour-supporting British Muslims for granted.

The truth is that Labour's problematic relationship with faith can hurt it among a variety of religious groups who believe that their faith-inspired family values are being underappreciated by a party which seems more interested in following the most culturally fashionable trends of the day. In the wake of the party's anti-Semitism crisis under Corbyn, its relationship with British Jewish communities is still in need of serious repair. The fact that at one point the 'anti-discrimination' and 'generous-spirited' Labour Party – once the natural political home of British Jews – was polling in single digits with this constituency in the build-up to the last general election will forever be a stain on its history.

In addition, Britain's thriving Hindu communities – aspirational, family-oriented hubs of academic excellence and entrepreneurial spirit that are awash with civic-minded associations that provide a sense of belonging – have increasingly lost respect for a Labour Party which many simply cannot relate to. Again, there is a serious need for the left to rebuild such relations – otherwise Labour will struggle to make much-needed gains in more affluent parts of inner London and fail to restore lost votes in places like Leicester. Embracing the traditional triad of faith, family and flag, and showing admiration for aspirational attitudes when it comes to educational attainment and socio-economic advancement, would go some way towards reconnecting with such lost and sceptical voters. With the right message of family-oriented aspiration and pro-enterprise values, Labour politicians – a good number of whom have traditional family backgrounds and impressive professional records themselves – could make headway with such communities and help their party eat into the number of Tory MPs in the capital.

There is another demographic that does not receive the attention it deserves in the field of psephology: British voters of black-African descent. The potential political leanings of members of these communities have too often been ignored by political commentators. The media have tended to treat Britain's black population as a monolithic bloc, ignoring the important cultural and social distinctions within it. This diverse section of the British electorate, which includes Christians of West African origin as well as more recently arrived Muslim refugees who have fled civil unrest in the Horn of Africa, is united by its shared appreciation of faith.

Brits of black-African descent are quite different to their co-racial Caribbean-origin counterparts living in the UK. According to the January 2021 poll by ICM Unlimited referred to above, nearly three in four British black-African respondents – 73 per cent – said that their religious identity was important to them. This dropped to just over half – 51 per cent – for British black-Caribbean respondents.[11] Indeed, it is not an uncommon sentiment in black-African communities – irrespective of ethnic background and religious affiliation – that one's devotion to God is best expressed by carrying out one's responsibilities towards one's own family. In my view, this is social conservatism at its very finest.

In the 2022 local English elections, Labour appeared to do rather well in London, taking control of Westminster, Wandsworth and Barnet councils from the Tories. But appearances can be deceptive. There is good reason to think that Labour lost some ground among ethnic-minority Londoners – especially the traditionally minded and upwardly mobile minority groups who could once be relied on to support it. Labour had an especially rude awakening in the south London borough of Croydon, where it lost the mayoral elections to the Conservatives and overall control of the council. The Tories gained four seats and are now just one councillor behind Labour. This is not the kind of outcome you would normally expect from a majority-non-white, multi-faith borough like this one.

There are many possible reasons for Labour's underwhelming performance in Croydon. The Labour administration's reputation for mismanagement may be one – Croydon council declared bankruptcy in 2020 and was, again, on the brink before the 2022 local elections. But there is another potential explanation: the high proportion of British black Africans (especially those of Christian faith) in the area. Given that the Church of England used to be known as the 'Tory Party at prayer', it could be argued that established Anglican communities of West African origin are therefore likely to be drawn to the Tories. Indeed, British Nigerian writer Tomiwa Owolade has argued that the 'inner cities will be the saviours of the Anglican Church' and that 'if you want a solid sense of the sacred, a connection to Britain's ancient Christian past, you are more likely to find it while eating jollof rice in a big tent in Kennington than eating a Yorkshire pudding in a small room in Harrogate'.[12]

Labour should be on high alert when it comes to black-African voters – the median Christian or Muslim voter of strong faith in this ethnic category is unlikely to embrace the kind of radical cultural liberalism which has taken hold of the left in recent times. To the contrary, such a voter is more likely to be seriously put off by it. In that sense, it is no surprise that a 2019 Runnymede Trust report co-authored by Omar Khan and Nicole Martin found that levels of support for the Conservative Party among black-African voters were on a consistently upward trajectory.[13] The reality is that in many inner-city neighbourhoods, and towns such as Luton, Milton Keynes or Swindon, as well as in parts of Essex such as Thurrock, Labour needs to shore up its relationship with voters of black-African descent, who tend to have a robust religious identity and regard their faith as an integral part of their everyday life.

Meanwhile, recent streams of Polish migration have injected considerable energy into Roman Catholicism in Britain – especially in Ealing in west London. There are now Romanian Orthodox churches dotted across London, in places such as Holborn, East Finchley and East Ham. It is worth noting that, according to the 2021 census, the 'White Other' category, mostly made up of Poles and Romanians, has gone from 4.4 per cent to 6.2 per cent of the population in England and Wales over the last decade.[14] While the hard-right myth that large-scale immigration explains the undermining of Britain's Christian identity continues to be peddled, the reality is that urban-based migrants originating from cities such as Lagos, Accra, Gdańsk and Cluj-Napoca are helping to sustain Christianity in England – a nation which has witnessed the rapid secularisation of its white-British mainstream. Labour should be a political home for ethnic-minority Christians with strong family values and a deep sense of justice.

Not for a second am I suggesting that the Labour Party should reinvent itself as an uncompromisingly socially conservative political outfit, one that should not challenge discrimination on the grounds of sexual orientation or gender reassignment – after all, these are both protected characteristics. But it should be aware that religious belief is also a protected characteristic under the 2010 Equality Act, passed by a Labour government. This, of course, muddies the water, meaning that Labour will have to address some admittedly difficult questions: what are the boundaries of free speech? When does perfectly legitimate criticism of beliefs cross into discriminatory territory? How does it balance diametrically opposed interests and reconcile incompatible beliefs that exist on the left? These are questions that even I find it tough to provide compelling answers for. And much of this is entirely Labour's doing, as over time it has recklessly attempted to build a coalition of ideologically disparate sectoral groups that all too often are neither representative nor accountable.

The best I can offer is that the contemporary British left has to foster a greater level of mutual tolerance and intellectual maturity in wider British society. (In truth, this may be challenging, as Labour hardly ranks highly on these fronts when it comes to its own parliamentary party.) Those who, for example, oppose same-sex marriage on the grounds of their religious beliefs are entitled to – but have to acknowledge that it is now legal in Britain and that as long as gay and lesbian people are behaving within the law, it is not the business of hard-line social conservatives to police what they do. Transgender people deserve respect and dignity – free from direct harassment, intimidation and violence on the grounds of their identities. Those who are responsible for such actions should meet the full force of the law. However, gender self-identification cannot become the norm in Britain, and those of faith are perfectly entitled to their conventional (some would say 'traditional' and 'outdated') understandings of what men and women are. They are also free to express concerns over the security and integrity of sensitive female-only spaces such as public toilets and changing rooms in the face of radical trans ideology.

People are within their rights to object to a biological male being able to freely enter such spaces, which should be designed to maximise the safety of women and their sense of security.

Labour must not allow a situation where many of Britain's ethnic-minority traditionalists of faith do not feel represented by the party. It cannot be seen as a political party which is largely uncomfortable with expressions of national pride, underappreciates the value of family stability, encourages individuals to see themselves as disempowered victims and entertains forms of radical transgenderism which threaten the integrity of sensitive female-only spaces.

As discussed, the Conservative Party has in recent years squandered the opportunity to take advantage of the widening disconnect between the left and traditional religious minorities by lurching into free-market libertarian territory – as was demonstrated by the brief leadership of Liz Truss – with little appreciation for the communitarian values of ethnic minorities who may be 'natural Tories' but are a world away from this political creed. It should also be noted that the Tories have their fair share of institutional and cultural problems. Recently charged with having an 'anti-Muslim sentiment' problem by the independent Singh investigation (led by Professor Swaran Singh), they continue to perform badly with British Muslim voters – even though the vast majority hail from robust family units, have a strong sense of community, and are appreciative of the religious freedoms afforded under their liberal democracy.[15] Tory MP Nusrat Ghani's claim in January 2022 that she was fired from a ministerial job because a party whip said her 'Muslimness' was making colleagues 'uncomfortable' is another setback for the Conservatives' relationship with British Muslims. A number of colleagues have jumped to her defence, including Nadhim Zahawi and Sajid Javid, as has the Labour mayor of London, Sadiq Khan. The Singh report, published in May 2021, which analysed almost 1,500 complaints, concluded that 'anti-Muslim sentiment remains a problem' within the Tory party.

The blunt truth is that for a supposedly civic-nationalist party, the Conservatives have not been sufficiently committed to fostering an inclusive notion of nationhood which is welcoming of decent and patriotic British Muslims. The Savanta ComRes pre-election poll of 2019 referred to earlier in this chapter found that only one in ten British Muslims intended to vote for the Tories, with six in ten saying they would vote for Labour.[16] The traditional triad of faith, family and flag is well and truly alive among anti-Islamist British Muslims, making it all the more striking that the Conservatives are still winning only a sliver of their electoral support. The Tories are missing out on a pool of traditional-minded minority voters who hold classically conservative values. Britain is not even close to having an authentically traditional centre-right party which understands the immense value of stable family units and broader collectivistic mindsets in modern British life. As it stands, resilient family-oriented minorities of faith are not particularly well represented by any mainstream British political party – but I remain hopeful that that will soon change.

In the build-up to the next general election, the left must shore up its relationship with traditional ethnic minorities by expressing a deeper appreciation of religion and spirituality – and, if it successfully manages to do so, the rewards could be great. If Labour was brave enough to make this point, it could well and truly claim to be the pro-minority party of twenty-first-century Britain. The biggest challenge for the Labour Party is to shift its status as a naturally 'pro-minority party' from the doom-and-gloom politics of victimhood to an uplifting narrative of celebration. When we consider family stability, intergenerational cohesion and the wholesomeness of faith, it is clear that there are ethnic-minority communities up and down the country which are anything but 'underprivileged' and 'disadvantaged'. Compared to their white-British peers, Indian-, Bangladeshi- and Pakistani-heritage children living in England are less likely to be raised in a lone-parent household. They, along with many of their peers of black-African descent, are more likely to be raised in a household with robust religious and cultural traditions that lay the foundations for a spiritual sense of meaning, and among local communities with civic associations and places of worship that function as sources of social belonging and rootedness.

Of course, the mainstream British left's political leadership must make more professional judgements about the kind of ultra-religious identity politics that reared its ugly head in traditionally Labour-voting Leicester. It must distance itself from religiously motivated organisations who do not have British social cohesion at heart, but are more interested in the currency of victimhood and in wrapping themselves with foreign territorial grievances which are mixed in with unquestionably religious tensions. Whether it is the Israeli–Palestinian conflict or Indian–Pakistani disputes over Kashmir, Labour must tread carefully: there are 'faith' associations operating in Britain which are only too happy to exploit these international issues to sow the seeds of division and spread hate in our country.

The emphasis needs to be on cultivating a wholesome social-democratic traditionalism which is rooted in family stability and community spirit – one that is able to harness the power of faith in the name of the national common good. After all, we shouldn't forget the important role played by places of worship and faith-based institutions in helping the UK government to provide public-health guidance to traditionally harder-to-reach sections of ethnic and religious minorities during the Covid-19 pandemic. These migrant-origin traditionalists are part of communities defined by their stable family structures and thriving civic assets, and are proud of the social, economic and cultural contributions they make in their country. They are the best of Britain – and it is time that the modern British left took a leaf out of the book of ethnic-minority patriots and better embraced inclusive feelings of national pride and loyalty.

5

BRITAIN'S ETHNIC-MINORITY PATRIOTS

In recent times, the Labour Party has been plunged into an internal culture war over matters of patriotism and national pride. For the especially grievance-fuelled sections of the modern British left, Britain is nothing less than a fundamentally racist society with a brutal imperialistic past – a country which has done and continues to do more harm than good. It is true that Britain must not rest on its laurels when it comes to strengthening equality of opportunity – ours is not a perfect meritocracy. There is no doubting that the British Empire was responsible for horrors that much of the general population are either unaware of or simply refuse to acknowledge (even though there is the all-important question of why some post-colonial nation states have fared much better than their counterparts after gaining independence from Britain). The key issue here is that the identitarian British left, all too often guilty of brainlessly importing US race politics, views racism and discrimination as a shared 'US–UK' problem, without taking into account very real historical, cultural and political differences between the two countries. The relatively youthful American experiment is failing; Britain remains a comparatively successful example of an established democracy – even after undergoing multiple processes of social and cultural transformation.

Dr Mariah Evans, co-author of a landmark study published in the journal *Frontiers in Sociology*, concluded that levels of prejudice towards minority groups in Britain are some of the lowest in the whole of Europe.[1] Indeed, little is said in 'progressive-liberal' circles about the fact that, when it comes to providing protections on the grounds of racial, ethnic and religious discrimination, Britain fares better than other diverse European democracies such as France, Germany and the Netherlands – something that aggressively anti-Brexit politicians on the British liberal left may find difficult to accept. Indeed, Britain is home to some of the most robust equality bodies in the Western world, with a range of 'protected characteristics' enshrined in the 2010 Equality Act passed by the Labour government, which remained in place during the prolonged period of Tory-led rule. In addition to this, Britain ranks highly when it comes to religious freedom, something which is much appreciated by its ethnic-minority communities of faith – especially first-generation migrants and refugees who may have fled their countries of origin due to sectarian violence or religiously driven persecution. Indeed, for all its flaws, Britain has a rich history of rehoming some of the world's most persecuted peoples – particularly relatively deprived communities who are simply not given the respect they deserve on this front.

The fact is that many of Britain's traditional ethnic-minority communities are poorly represented by elements of the modern left who are either ignorant of their patriotic sentiments or opportunistically foisting their anti-British prejudices onto them in the name of 'social justice'. I would go so far as to say that, at times, traditional ethnic minorities are exploited by the identitarian left in the name of race-baiting opportunism and their pseudo-revolutionary games – especially in the spheres of politics and the media. Much of the liberal-left's political analysis views matters of fairness and equality through the prism of race alone – and, all too often, the woeful conclusion reached is that Britain's social institutions and economic system are deliberately rigged against ethnic minorities. This is a myth that is peddled with impunity. In truth, the country is awash with thriving ethnic-minority communities who are appreciative of the opportunities, protections and freedoms which are provided in one of the most tolerant, anti-discrimination, pro-equality democracies on earth. This should be celebrated by the modern left – indeed, Britain would not be in such a position if it weren't for Labour politicians with a strong sense of fairness and justice, true progressive stalwarts who were responsible for passing the race-relations legislation of the 1970s as well as the landmark 2010 Equality Act, which

131

underlined race, ethnicity and religious belief as protected characteristics.

In recent times, the Labour Party leadership has somewhat smelt the coffee and woken up to the fact that it must address its 'patriotism deficit' – something that is off-putting not only for the white working classes in their pro-Brexit, post-industrial heartlands, but also for traditional ethnic minorities with a strong sense of Britishness who live in the inner cities. However, Labour's mild expressions of patriotism have been met with serious pushback from the left. An especially questionable charge, made by the likes of Aditya Chakrabortty in *The Guardian*, is that embracing expressions of British patriotism would alienate ethnic minorities.[2] Taj Ali argued in *The Independent* that Labour is in danger of alienating 'ethnic-minority voters' by appealing to 'nationalists'. Responding to the party's attempted patriotic rebranding, Ali suggested that 'Labour should avoid adopting right-wing nationalist rhetoric'.[3] This is the same kind of language that many on the left used to disparage the vote for Brexit – baselessly presenting it as a white-nostalgic enterprise in the culturally backward provinces. And yet many ethnic minorities in urban areas voted Leave.

Ali, like me, is a Lutonian. Luton is a post-industrial town where less than half of the population is white British. In the June 2016 referendum on EU membership, Luton returned a Leave vote of 56.5 per cent. Many ethnic-minority voters here supported Brexit for a variety of reasons, such as a desire for greater national control over the immigration system. Many community elders I've spoken to in my home town voted to leave because they had reservations about free movement with less developed EU member states where bigoted attitudes towards ethnic and religious minorities are perceived to be more mainstream. To be quite blunt, neither Chakrabortty nor Ali is representative of the patriotic sentiments which run deep in many of Britain's communities of South Asian heritage.

Another of *The Guardian*'s grievance manufacturers, Nesrine Malik, has also revealed her upset over patriotic noises from the Labour Party. The 'new management' in the post-Corbyn era will cost ethnic-minority votes, she has claimed.[4] Malik says that by emphasising patriotism and moving to the right on cultural issues, Labour risks losing not only mass ethnic-minority support, but also its soul. According to this view, the 'BAME community' has little or no sense of national pride or appreciation of British life. This assumption is both misguided and divisive.

A notable section of Britain's non-white population moved directly to the UK from unstable parts of the world with dysfunctional political systems and substandard public infrastructure. Part of the reason my Bangladeshi-origin parents decided to establish themselves in Britain was the stable nature of British democratic society and the great educational opportunities on offer for their children. This feeds into a naturally positive orientation towards Britain – a country that provided them with an opportunity to start afresh and prosper. I was born and raised in Britain, so why shouldn't I feel that I owe a great deal to my country? Having been state-educated up to the age of 18, having had my doctorate comprehensively sponsored by the Economic and Social Research Council (ESRC) and having been blessed with exciting economic opportunities, of course I feel grateful. Add the fact that there are ethnic and religious minorities persecuted all over the world, then there surely ought to be some kind of appreciation for the robust pro-equality legal framework that Britain has in place, one underpinned by comprehensive anti-discrimination protections and regulations.

The progressive-activist brigade, which lectures Labour on how to engage with Britain's ethnic-minority people, fails to understand that patriotic sentiments and culturally traditional values run deep in many British non-white communities. Arguing that Labour should steer clear of expressions of patriotism and national civic pride, on the baseless grounds that it would alienate swathes of 'BAME' people, is nonsense. It is an attempt to ensure that the party continues to indulge in racial identity politics, and to support the kind of radical cultural liberalism that runs counter to traditional family-oriented values which define many non-white communities of faith across the home nations.

Many white working-class voters in the so-called 'Red Wall' – who abandoned Labour for the Conservatives in the 2019 general election – have a strong British identity, are family-oriented and want immigration controls and tougher action on antisocial behaviour in local neighbourhoods. But anyone who thinks these values are only shared by white voters does not understand ethnic-minority Britain very well at all. If those in the London-based media sector want to meet fiercely patriotic, family-oriented Brits, they do not need to visit a pub in Bolsover or a working men's club in Sedgefield – they just need to take a short trip to the minority places of worship and thriving civic associations on their doorsteps. But identitarian leftists would prefer to pretend that all ethnic minorities support the same mixture of open-borders cosmopolitanism and racial identity politics that they do.

Britain's progressive activists – who span various spheres of British life, from politics to academia to the media and entertainment – are far from being ideologically in sync with mainstream ethnic-minority public opinion. While these progressive activists squirm at the quietest expressions of patriotism, a comfortable majority of non-white people attach importance to their British national identity. Many of Britain's non-white people – who can trace their ancestral origins back to countries with autocratic regimes and rampant political oppression – simply do not share in this domestic progressive-liberal discontent. And while progressive activists look to 'protect' an imaginary 'BAME community' from the forces of oppression, they fail to acknowledge that non-white people tend to be more satisfied with their life in the UK than their white

peers – one of the key findings of a nationally representative poll carried out by ICM Unlimited in January
2021.[5] Progressive activists are either unaware of the culturally conservative attitudes in non-white communities
or, worse, are fully aware of them but would still rather
exploit ethnic minorities to promote their identitarian
agenda. This tribe of left-wingers – instinctively hostile
to expressions of patriotism, dissatisfied with the democratic system and always keen to interpret a range of
social issues through the prism of race – threatens to lock
Labour in a position of never-ending electoral misery and
psychological pessimism if they get their way.

A patriotic pitch which understands the significance of
family and appreciates a desire for stable local communities could command considerable cross-ethnic appeal in
Britain. Framing this as courting the 'white-nationalist
vote' is both divisive and ignorant of the patriotism which
runs deep in non-white communities across Britain. And
if such unpatriotic thinking continues to wield considerable influence on the left, Labour will be able to offer
nothing more than a miserable form of grievance politics,
which is likely to prove very costly at the ballot box. The
lessons of the 2019 general election must be learnt.

One of the more recent in-depth explorations of British
national identity was the aforementioned ICM Unlimited
poll, in which sharp political divides along party lines
emerged. While 83 per cent of Conservative voters in the
2019 general election said that their British national identity was important to them, this shot down to 57 per cent

for Labour voters. While only 16 per cent of Conservative voters said that their British national identity was not important to them, 40 per cent of Labour voters did so.[6] These party divides in the 'Johnson v. Corbyn' general election were not a surprise. Much of this division was driven by pro-Brexit voters in working-class constituencies who usually voted for Labour but shifted to the Tories. This movement was principally driven by the need to facilitate the UK's departure from the EU, but also by the fact that their natural party was far detached from voters' quietly traditional values and sense of national pride.

Arguably the most interesting conclusion of this poll was that there exists fertile ground for the cultivation and consolidation of a civic British identity which is open to a variety of racial identities, ethnic backgrounds and religious affiliations. While we have been bombarded by misguided narratives which suggest that Labour will alienate swathes of ethnic-minority voters by embracing symbols of Britishness such as the Union flag and other forms of patriotic expression, the data provides a very different story indeed. ICM found that while 63 per cent of white people in the UK felt British national identity was important to them, this rose by five percentage points (to 68 per cent) for their non-white counterparts.[7] While one in three white people felt British national identity was not important to them, this dropped to only one in four for non-white people. Yes, you read that right – in modern Britain, a non-white adult is more likely than a white peer to view their British national identity as an important element of their individual identity, and a white adult is more likely than a non-white peer to say the opposite.

Why is it the case that white people in Britain are less likely to place importance on their British national identity when compared to their non-white compatriots? In my view, there are two important trends to consider in this context. One is what I consider to be an 'elite anti-Britishness' in metropolitan white-collar sections of the mainstream population. This usually consists of well-resourced white Brits in affluent neighbourhoods who typically vote for non-Tory 'progressive' options. Viewing themselves as 'outward-looking internationalists', they are perhaps still reeling from the fact that the UK voted to leave the EU and then awarded 'Brexit Boris' with the largest Conservative majority since the 1987 general election. These are liberal-left types who fail to see much good in Britain – believing that it is a largely reactionary and prejudiced society where ethnic and racial minorities are in need of far greater rights and protections. They are more 'cosmopolitan' in terms of sense of belonging and general world view – more like 'citizens of the earth' than people with an attachment to a traditional notion of nationhood.

The second trend is more 'separatist' in nature – white Brits who are far more attached to English, Scottish or Welsh identities, respectively. This will include socially conservative 'Blukippers' and those who vote for 'pro-independence' parties such as the Scottish National Party (SNP) or Plaid Cymru. Bonded by their anti-Westminster sentiments, their loyalties are primarily with their respective 'home nation', with little space for 'British' identity alongside this form of identification. But with nearly seven in ten non-white people – along with more than six in ten white people – reporting that their British national identity is important to their existence, there is clearly room for an inclusive, multiracial Britishness to be harnessed and embedded in civil society. The left's embracing of the Union flag and adoption of patriotic expressions of Britishness is not going to lead to the desertion from the Labour Party of swathes of ethnic-minority voters – if anything, it will help to arrest their growing flirtation with the Conservatives.

What is certainly not being learnt by much of the left is that English patriotism is not rooted in ancestral notions of nationhood and various forms of xenophobia. Sending both the liberal left and far right into a tailspin, recent survey figures show that support for a more open and inclusive English identity has strengthened in recent years. Now only slightly more than 10 per cent of people believe that ethnicity is an important factor in determining Englishness, a drop from 20 per cent in a decade. Interestingly, the drop has been particularly sharp among those over the age of 65 – a section of the population often smeared as backward and regressive. From 2012, the importance of 'whiteness' to English identity among this demographic has dropped from 35 to 16 per cent.[8] It is true that holding a stronger English identity was associated with a higher likelihood of voting Leave in the

2016 referendum on EU membership, but to suggest that Brexit was a provincial English enterprise fuelled by racist sentiments and 'white nostalgia' is wide of the mark. It is a fundamental misrepresentation of the mainstream civic framings of Englishness and the socio-political drivers of Brexit.

For most people, Englishness is far more about doing your bit, with more than 70 per cent believing that making social and economic contributions is an important element of English identity.[9] The data challenges the perception that the UK's decision to leave the EU reflected the rise of a xenophobic English identity, framed in exclusivist, ancestral terms; in fact, the findings show that people increasingly view Englishness in ethnically inclusive terms.

I would also offer the view that the sheer richness of English heritage and culture is a cornerstone of a civic Englishness that seamlessly incorporates the nation's diverse population – without compromising the solidarity of the Union. This includes admiration for the jaw-dropping magnificence of English Gothic architecture, appreciating the creation of Magna Carta at Runnymede (something that has personal significance for me as a Royal Holloway alumnus) and celebrating ground-breaking English achievements during the Industrial Revolution. Chaucer, Shakespeare, Chesterton, Dickens, the Brontë sisters, Austen, Kipling, Orwell, Woolf, Christie, and many others – the list of magnificent writers produced by England is remarkable. Ours is also a nation with a strong sporting heritage – with sports such as football, cricket, field hockey, lawn tennis and rugby union having been codified by the English. Indeed, England's national teams in football and cricket are incredibly diverse – with contemporary Caribbean-origin stars such as footballer Raheem Sterling and cricketer Jofra Archer being first-generation migrants.

The successes of our football team – a multiracial squad which included players who can trace their origins back to countries such as Jamaica, Barbados, Nigeria and the Republic of Ireland – during Euro 2020 spurred on the fostering of an uplifting, inclusive Englishness. A study by think tank British Future found that two-thirds of people see the English football team as a national symbol that belongs to people of every race and ethnic background.[10] Just one in 13 people disagreed. And it was wonderful to see the Euro 2020 #EnglandTogether campaign bring together a diverse array of organisations, such as the Mosques and Imams National Advisory Board (MINAB), JW3 (also known as the Jewish Community Centre London), City Sikhs and leading British Asian newspaper *Eastern Eye*, in their collective support of our national team.

All too often, mainstream commentary on England and English identity has been in the business of peddling simplistic caricatures. While other forms of patriotism on these islands have been celebrated as progressive and inclusive, English identity has been repeatedly derided as reactionary and divisive. The St George's flag has been unfairly treated as a symbol of exclusionary nationalism and imperial nostalgia. But this is more of a reflection of the anti-English biases of metropolitan political elitists and self-hating 'intellectuals' than of the realities on the ground, which provide a far more positive picture.

There has been an absence of mainstream political leadership in developing an inclusive, values-based English identity, one that can strengthen the bonds of social trust and mutual respect between England's racial and ethnic groups. This inclusive patriotism could celebrate English contributions towards scientific advancement and the arts, and tell uplifting stories of how post-war migrants from different parts of the world joined forces with the existing population to help rebuild England after the devastation of the Second World War. The contemporary British left should be in the business of championing a modern conception of English nationhood which is rooted in family-orientedness, civic duty and equality of opportunity. We must never allow the divisive identitarian fringes of society to seize the narrative when it comes to the meaning of Englishness and what England represents. This inclusive, cross-ethnic English sense of pride is something to be harnessed, not overlooked due to anxieties that it will alienate the other home nations (who have admittedly been more successful in cultivating open and incorporative national identities).

The association often made between British Euroscepticism and xenophobia is dubious to say the least – as is the association between pro-EU feeling and inclusivity: a 2018 study found that people of black-African descent faced 'widespread and entrenched prejudice and exclusion' across the EU, and that the UK had one of the lowest levels of reported race-related harassment and violence in the 12-country study. (In this context, it is worth noting that the overwhelming majority of Brits of black-African descent live in England.) Roughly one in three of the respondents to the study said they had experienced some form of racial harassment in the past five years, while only 21 per cent of respondents in the UK said they had. In Finland, the corresponding figure was 63 per cent.[11] In this context, it is worth noting that while there are still occasional instances of racism towards black footballers in England, they are nowhere near as frequent as in other parts of Europe. It is true that Marcus Rashford, Jadon Sancho and Bukayo Saka received a torrent of online racist abuse after missing their penalties in the Euro 2020 final defeat against Italy, but the vast majority of this originated from foreign-based accounts. The highest rates of racist violence were reported in Finland (14 per cent), closely followed by Austria and the Republic of Ireland (13 per cent each). The figure among UK respondents was 3 per cent.[12]

These survey figures strongly discredit two common but deeply questionable claims: that English identity is increasingly being framed in ethno-racially exclusivist terms, and that English xenophobia itself drives British Euroscepticism. The figures are a blow both to those on the liberal left who depict Englishness as an exclusionary, narrow-minded identity, and to a hard-right faction who believe that having a certain racial and ethnic ancestral background is integral to Englishness. Neither, it seems, is actually representative of the views of the English public at large. Professor John Denham, a former Labour MP and a leading authority when it comes to research on English identity, said: 'The idea that English is an ethnic identity is widely repeated in the media and politics... Ethnicity is clearly much less important outside a small hardcore of residents. The further development of an inclusive Englishness would benefit from positive engagement by leaders across the political spectrum.'[13]

Interestingly, the subject of Englishness brings together an unlikely alliance of the liberal left and the far right. *Guardian* writer and economist Paul Mason declared in 2015 that he did not want to be English, and that 'any attempt to create an English identity will fail' – and who could forget Emily Thornberry, who snobbishly tweeted out a photo of a house in Rochester draped in English flags with a white van parked in the drive.[14] On the flip side, we have organisations such as the English Defence League (EDL) – established in my home town of Luton – which has tried its utmost to take ownership of the English flag through its divisive and inflammatory rhetoric. We are subjected to the incoherent ramblings of rabble-rousing frauds such as Tommy Robinson (real name Stephen Yaxley-Lennon), who advertise themselves as 'true patriots' but are ultimately focused on stoking community tensions in the name of individual gain.

Neither the liberal left nor the far right is remotely interested in cultivating a positive, uplifting, optimistic Englishness based on shared values and common purpose, one that is family-oriented and community-spirited, emphasises the value of hard work and promotes equality of opportunity – an Englishness that understands the importance of human relationships and encourages social responsibility. And, most crucially, one that firmly rejects the divisiveness that comes with identity politics.

But this is precisely what has developed. I was raised in Luton and spent my entire spell in further education at Royal Holloway in the Surrey town of Egham. I have interacted with both working-class, dyed-in-the-wool Labour voters and middle-class, socially conservative Tories in decent numbers – two constituencies who are generally united by a dedicated work ethic, strong family values and deep sense of patriotism. Despite being of South Asian origin, I have never once encountered hostility or even funny looks when expressing my love for England. In fact, the opposite has been the case – it is those shared bonds of affection and the comfort found in common values which are integral to tying together England's people.

Similarly, we should reject narratives which suggest that ethnic-minority people are intimidated by patriotic expressions of Britishness (or, indeed, Englishness). Britain has not fared badly at all in cultivating an inclusive national identity that people of different backgrounds can relate to and buy into – something that should be viewed as the success it undoubtedly is. We should be aware of the impact of tribal identity politics and secessionist agendas on sections of the population with weak attachments to British national identity. Radical ideologues – political Islamists, far-right nativists and hard-left identitarians – thrive in the absence of attachments to shared, inclusive identities rooted in nationhood, and we should strive to counter such divisive agendas through shared values and a sense of common purpose. The moderate left must challenge hard-left identitarians who portray Britain as a fundamentally racist country with a major anti-Muslim problem – something that in turn feeds political Islamists who are not remotely interested in fostering social cohesion. Rather, they are focused on introducing Islamic-inspired regulations of the British public sphere, as well as promoting a toxic religio-political creed that abhors the democratic nation state. This 'red–green alliance' must be marginalised by the mainstream British left if it wishes to strengthen its appeal among the country's many ethnic-minority patriots.

The patronising infantilisation of non-white people who have established themselves in Britain, taken advantage of the opportunities provided in one of the fairest democratic societies on earth and raised successful children (many of whom are now outperforming their white-British peers on a number of social and economic metrics), will backfire spectacularly. What may help is talking more about family and education. Not the 'race-conscious education' that views the promotion of self-discipline and routine as reactionary, but rather a social policy that places families at its heart and relentlessly promotes educational excellence – academic and vocational – as the basis for broad-based prosperity. What may also shore up the modern British left's relationship with traditional ethnic minorities is showing a greater appreciation of faith and how one's religious beliefs can be a source of resilience, self-discipline and optimism.

One institution that provides the perfect fulcrum for a quietly traditional patriotism which can cut across race, ethnicity and religion, but that is often vilified by left-wing identitarians obsessed with race and empire, is the royal family. Her Majesty Queen Elizabeth II's magnificent seven-decade reign was characterised by an unwavering sense of duty and unshakeable commitment to public service. Indeed, she embodied qualities that are perhaps not as fashionable as they ought to be – grace, stoicism, determination and restraint. In an increasingly secular, individualistic age, the Queen stood for family, community and faith, values that go down especially well with traditionally minded communities, many of whom see the monarchy not as outdated, but as a welcome corrective to the turpitude of our times. Far from being out of touch, the Queen embodied values that were very much shared by many of those she reigned over, which is why, after her death on 8 September 2022, she was mourned with such intensity by so very many of our compatriots, of all faiths and ethnicities.

There has been much – in my view simplistic – talk of the royal family being a tired and anachronistic institution which is fundamentally detached from 'modern Britain'. I couldn't disagree more with this evaluation. Her Majesty's balancing of loyalty to her traditional values and embrace of significant forms of domestic and international change positioned her especially well with Britain's ethnic and religious minorities. Indeed, it was wonderful to see Union flag bunting across my multi-ethnic, religiously diverse home town of Luton during the Platinum Jubilee celebrations of 2022. The traditional triad of faith, family and flag is well and truly alive in this town – whose demographically heterogeneous communities were tied together by a shared appreciation of our longest-serving monarch's inspirational devotion to her people.

Queen Elizabeth II deserves great credit for the part she played in fostering a confident multi-ethnic democracy in the post-Empire world. As a British Muslim with an ethnically mixed heritage that can be traced back to two Commonwealth states – Bangladesh and India – I firmly believe that Her Majesty invested great time and energy in strengthening this important political association of nations and territories. She smoothed Britain's transition from imperial power to much-respected member of the postcolonial international system – she was a symbol of unity and constancy who helped to shape Britain into the confident, multi-ethnic, post-Empire democracy it is today. And nowhere was that better reflected than in the sheer diversity that characterised both 'the Queue' for Her

Majesty's lying-in-state and the roadside crowds who paid their respects on the day of her funeral. Consequently, hearing rent-a-gob commentators claiming that the Queen was somehow responsible for the evils of colonialism has been most jarring – such assertions are both socially divisive and historically illiterate.

King Charles III has begun his reign in the inclusive spirit of his mother. Despite being the head of the Church of England, he has referred to himself as the 'defender of all faiths' and declared his belief that Britain is 'a community of communities'. These are not the words of a man leading a fundamentally racist institution, but rather the sentiments of a traditional figurehead who values cohesion and inclusivity. One could even say that this is the British monarchy's 'progressive conservatism' in all its glory.

Indeed, it is Britain's 'progressive conservatism' – its appreciation of its own cultural heritage and embrace of significant domestic and international change – that makes it the successful integration story it is today. The rich tapestry of modern-day Britain includes ethnic-minority patriots who are all too often woefully represented by identitarian leftists and anti-monarchist toy-town revolutionaries who fail to appreciate the success of their own country. It is a land of generosity and opportunity where ethnic-minority communities – especially those with stable family structures, thriving civic assets and a strong sense of national belonging – make remarkable social, economic and cultural contributions to their country. While the doom-and-gloom merchants of the grievance-manufacturing industry continue to peddle fundamental untruths about Britain, the reality is that it is one of the most successful examples of a hyper-diverse democracy in the modern world.

6

BRITAIN'S ETHNIC MINORITIES AND THEIR DEMOCRACY

The debate on Britain's hyper-diverse democracy can be somewhat polarising at times. There are some who believe that British democracy is fundamentally flawed – a failing system that is deliberately rigged against its own ethnic minorities. I call this political tribe 'the obsessives of the left': those who tend to interpret forms of ethnic-minority underperformance and disadvantage through the prism of racial discrimination, either in ignorance of, or deliberately overlooking, other factors that have little to nothing to do with racism. They risk dragging the Labour Party down a road of all too often presenting a variety of racial inequalities in a reckless and divisive manner – ignoring influential determinants such as family structure, community norms, social class and geography. Then we have the 'denialists of the right' – in their view, the job is well and truly done when it comes to tackling racial discrimination in Britain. If there are ethnic minorities who are lagging behind, 'denialists' will offer the view that it must have absolutely nothing to do with forms of identity-based prejudice. Here exists a romanticisation of Britain – considered as the perfect model of race relations where little or nothing can be done to improve its multiracial, religiously diverse democracy.

Interestingly, there have been times when I have been accused by various actors of falling into each of these camps. I do unapologetically hold the view that Britain remains one of the most successful examples of a multi-ethnic, religiously diverse democracy in the modern world. When it comes to the existence of robust laws outlawing discrimination on the grounds of race, ethnicity or religion, Britain is one of the leading countries in the industrialised Western world, outperforming major EU member states such as France, Germany, the Netherlands, Spain and Italy, along with Commonwealth partners such as Australia and New Zealand. The UK also manages its current-day racial heterogeneity far better than the United States of America, with its vastly different history of electoral enfranchisement and civil liberties. This was the conclusion reached in the landmark 2000 Parekh report (ironically for the think tank that commissioned it, the Runnymede Trust, which is now at the heart of Britain's grievance-manufacturing industry) – and few would argue that this is no longer the case.[1] The March 2021 Sewell report authored by the UK government's Commission on Race and Ethnic Disparities (CRED) concluded that the success of ethnic-minority communities in the sphere of education (and to a lesser extent, the economy) means that Britain 'should be regarded as a model for other White-majority countries'.[2]

The only advanced industrial democracy that can claim to be more successful than the UK in terms of 'diversity management' is Canada, which traditionally outperforms the UK when it comes to social cohesion, national sense of belonging and public confidence in the democratic system of governance. In this context, it must be acknowledged that Canada has a relatively selective immigration system and a smaller national population spread over a far greater land mass. The Henry Jackson Society's Index of National Resilience, published in September 2020, placed Canada as the leading country in the 'D-10' (the G7 plus Australia, India and South Korea) for 'national identity and belonging' and 'quality of law and order' – with the country also ranking highly for other measures of 'societal resilience' such as 'altruism' and 'national happiness/public optimism'.[3] In cultivating a pan-Canadian civic identity inspired by the 1982 Charter of Rights and Freedoms, the multi-ethnic and multi-lingual Canadian federation has become an impressive example of a diverse democracy in the post-Second World War era that is in relatively strong shape in terms of institutional and societal resilience (in spite of some admittedly shoddy political 'leadership' in recent times in the shape of the truly insufferable Justin Trudeau).

But what do ethnic-minority people make of British democracy and how satisfied are they with their lives in modern society? Well, it depends on which ethnic-minority group you are referring to (and indeed, which section within that group). This nuance is all too often missing in conversations on the contemporary British left about our democracy and the general quality of race relations. The ESRC-funded Ethnic Minority British Election Survey (EMBES), conducted in the aftermath of the 2010 general election, remains the largest full-scale study into ethnic-minority public attitudes and socio-political behaviour conducted in the UK.[4] It comprehensively covered the social and political behaviour and attitudes of the five largest established ethnic categories in the UK – Indian, Pakistani, Bangladeshi, black Caribbean and black African – and was one of the most rigorous investigations ever held into the socio-political incorporation of ethnic minorities in an advanced liberal democracy. It showed that black Caribbeans – the most established ethnic-minority group in terms of resettlement in the UK – lagged considerably behind the other four non-white groupings when it came to being satisfied with British democracy, being notably less likely to be satisfied (48 per cent).[5] The 2010 survey also identified that the level of democratic satisfaction within the black-African group was closer to that within the three South Asian groups than to that among their co-racial black-Caribbean counterparts, highlighting significant between-group variation within the 'black-British' population. The three South Asian groups reported the highest levels of satisfaction with Britain's democratic system – with people of Bangladeshi descent being the most satisfied with how democracy functions in the UK (79 per cent).[6] Britain's Bangladeshi- and Pakistani-heritage groups – two predominantly Sunni Muslim groups – reported the highest levels of democratic satisfaction and were the most likely to hold a high level of trust in both Parliament and politicians in general.[7]

There was a clear intergenerational difference in democratic satisfaction among the respondents, with first-generation migrants being more satisfied with the way democracy works in the UK. Seventy-eight per cent of first-generation migrants reported that they were either 'very satisfied' or 'fairly satisfied' with Britain's democratic system. The corresponding figure for their British-born descendants was just 53 per cent.[8] While only 7 per cent of first-generation migrants stated that they were 'very dissatisfied' with British democracy, the corresponding figure for ethnic-minority people born in the UK was more than double, at 15 per cent.[9] With a notable proportion of ethnic-minority people born abroad, socialisation under less stable and undemocratic political cultures in the country of origin can lead to more positive orientations towards more democratic 'host' systems.

This view suggests that early life experience of repressive, autocratic regimes may produce positive socio-political outcomes in the host country, as individuals raised in such environments may have a greater appreciation of democratic rights and the ability to influence politics. It also suggests that British-born second-, third- and indeed fourth-generation migrants are more likely to have stronger expectations of British democracy than their first-generation 'elders', who have a history of living under far harsher political, social and economic environments abroad. This means that expectations of fairness and equality may differ as migrants become more generationally integrated – something that Britain will have to bear in mind as its multiracial society evolves over time.

What is clear is that, just over a decade ago, the most sophisticated, full-scale survey into the public attitudes of British ethnic minorities ever carried out found that, in terms of institutional trust, these groups differed a great deal in how they viewed the prevailing system of governance, and that, as a broader population, ethnic-minority Brits were notably more likely to be satisfied with democratic politics than the white-British mainstream (69 per cent against 62 per cent).[10] In an era in which the acronym 'BAME' has been used extensively to signify an imaginary non-white collective which is politically disaffected and systemically victimised, these figures suggested the very opposite (even though it is worth noting that second- and third-generation non-white migrants are comparatively less satisfied with British democracy than their parents and grandparents, as they are more integrated into the relatively cynical white-British majority).

Fresher data supports the finding that traditional ethnic minorities demonstrate higher levels of democratic satisfaction and institutional trust – especially when it comes to the predominantly non-white British Muslim population. In September 2021, the twentieth anniversary of the 9/11 Islamist terrorist attacks, I asked myself the following very important question: did the so-called 'War on Terror' and heightened domestic security measures have a destructive impact on the democratic satisfaction felt by British Muslims and their relationship with public institutions?

Well, the picture is far more positive than some may think – and built on the generally positive findings on democratic satisfaction and institutional trust from the 2010 EMBES. According to a 2020 study by Crest Advisory, more than three in four British Muslims believe that Britain is a good place to live as a Muslim.[11] The main reason for this is the freedoms afforded to them to practise their faith. Interestingly, a far lower proportion of non-Muslims – 52 per cent – think Britain is a good place to live as a Muslim. Perhaps this is an indication that the view of Britain as 'Islamophobic' is far more prevalent among the non-Muslim mainstream than among Muslims themselves. This follows on from earlier studies which showed that even though many British Muslims have opposed military interventions involving the UK – such as the 2003 invasion of Iraq – they have remained largely satisfied with the way in which democracy works in Britain.

There are also encouraging figures about the relationship between British Muslims and domestic law-and-order institutions. The Crest Advisory study found that while 51 per cent of the wider public feel that the police engage well with their community, this rises to 53 per cent for British Muslims.[12] Britain's Bangladeshi-origin population – one I belong to – is overwhelmingly Sunni Muslim. In the most recent crime survey for England and Wales, people of Bangladeshi origin were more likely to have confidence in their local police force than white Brits (81 per cent and 74 per cent, respectively).[13] Furthermore, as noted in Chapter 2, while some have accused the UK's counterterrorism strategy, Prevent, of alienating the 'British Muslim community', Crest Advisory found that the majority of British Muslims – 56 per cent – are not even aware of it. On matters of public safety, 63 per cent of British Muslims say they're worried about the threat of Islamist extremism – not too dissimilar to the figure of 67 per cent for the general population.[14] Two-thirds of British Muslims say they would refer concerns about radicalisation to the government's counterterrorism pro-gramme – which is actually higher than the corresponding figure for the broader public (63 per cent).[15]

British Muslims – the vast majority of whom belong to non-white ethnic minorities – are not the put-upon vic-tims of Islamophobia that the identitarian lobby portrays them as. Nor are Muslims part of a disloyal 'fifth column', as is claimed by anti-Muslim bigots. In reality, British Muslims have been let down by rabid ideologues – both Islamist extremists and identitarian grievance-mongers – who thrive on sowing the seeds of social division. I have never shied away from discussing the serious internal problems within British Muslim communities. But

Britain's mainly patriotic and dutiful Muslims do not deserve to be collectively tarnished by the actions of religious zealots, and it is time to stop making unfounded generalisations about entire social groups.

While British society and many of its institutions have recently been vilified over matters of fairness and opportunity, our country is home to some of the strongest equality bodies in the world, and has a far stronger degree of institutional tolerance than much of the EU. Indeed, the European Court of Justice (ECJ) – the highest court of the EU – ruled in July 2021 that businesses have the right to ban Muslim employees from wearing the hijab if they work face to face with customers or if it causes workplace conflicts and tensions. In a binding ruling that would apply in all 27 member states, judges decided that prohibiting the wearing of any visible expression of political, philosophical or religious belief in the workplace 'may be justified by the employer's need to present a neutral image towards customers or to prevent social disputes'.[16]

Some may argue that this form of 'muscular liberalism' encourages social integration. I couldn't disagree more. This is a deeply illiberal ruling that fundamentally infringes on religious freedom and, on the contrary, undermines the integration of Muslims into European society. The countries of Europe should be seeking to promote rather than inhibit the labour-market integration of hijab-wearing female Muslim citizens, many of whom may live in relatively deprived communities, and for whom work would mean greater economic self-sufficiency and personal independence. Finding employment in the mainstream economy also provides Muslim women with an opportunity to engage more with members of the general population, outside their own religious communities. Moreover, the hijab, unlike the niqab, does not actually present a facial barrier to interpersonal communication. To argue that it does, as the ECJ seems to, is simply misleading.

Similarly, the perception of the UK as a bigoted and inward-looking island and of mainland Europe as an oasis of tolerance and openness isn't borne out by the facts. While the left-wing grievance-mongers and Islamist organisations of the 'red–green' alliance wish to caricature Britain as an aggressively 'Islamophobic' place, the views of the majority of ordinary British Muslims suggest otherwise. In the post-9/11 world, British Muslims are not the oppressed and disaffected group some may think. Many belong to strong family units and well-bonded communities which are appreciative of the religious freedoms and anti-discrimination protections provided under British democracy. In the interests of national solidarity and social cohesion, therefore, we must push back against this anti-British alliance of hard-left ideologues and political Islamists – an unholy coalition that crassly portrays itself as representative of British Muslims. And 'progressive liberals' should be cautious about being sucked into this divisive partnership. The doom-and-gloom narratives peddled by the anti-British brigade must be robustly challenged by decent-hearted patriots of all faiths and ethnicities.

While the stronger forms of political disaffection and life dissatisfaction can be found in black-British communities, it is vital that the phrase 'black-British community' be consigned to the dustbin of history – it is nothing but a fictitious social construct which does not reflect the reality on the ground. Black Britons do not represent a singular monocultural bloc that sings from the same hymn sheet, with two sizeable co-racial groups – black-British Africans and black-British Caribbeans – being vastly different in terms of their political attitudes and social behaviour. A 2021 report for the Henry Jackson Society found that the former are notably more positive about the current state of UK race relations and less likely to think that we live in a fundamentally racist society than British black Caribbeans.[17] As well as being more likely to attach importance to their religious identities, black-British Africans are less likely to say that they had unstable family lives during their childhoods – and, crucially, more likely to report satisfaction with their lives in Britain.[18] This supports previous work on institutional trust which shows that black-British Africans, when compared with black-British Caribbeans, are far more likely to have confidence in their local police force and report satisfaction with British democracy.[19]

What could account for some of these differences? Frame of reference is likely to play its part. Black-British Caribbeans, a community that has been in the UK for longer, originate from relatively stable nation states with multi-party parliamentary democracies. This certainly isn't the case for black-British Africans, who are comparative more recently arrived as a group. Given that some originate from relatively unstable countries characterised by severe political oppression and intense societal fractionalisation, it is no surprise if they have a naturally positive orientation towards British democracy and UK race relations. Thus it is high time to separate out the culturally diverse black-British population, and to use this understanding to inform both our social policy and our broader political discourse – especially when we look at public trust and confidence in the police.

There have been numerous reports published in the aftermath of race riots which have made policy recommendations to help improve interethnic and police–community relations. For instance, the findings of the Scarman report, commissioned by the government to investigate the disorder in Brixton in 1981, stated that the riots were the by-product of 'complex political, social, and economic factors', and that urgent action needed to be taken to prevent 'racial disadvantage' becoming an 'endemic, ineradicable disease'.[20] It suggested that changes in police and law-enforcement training needed to be made, inspiring the passage of the 1984 Police and Criminal Evidence Act. However, proposed economic and social reforms (which included the introduction of positive action to address racial disadvantage) were left largely unimplemented by Margaret Thatcher's government.

In modern Britain, there remains much room for improvement when it comes to police–community relations. Nearly three in five black Britons believe that their local police force treats their racial group unfairly. In addition to this, the majority disagree with the view that the UK does not have a problem with police brutality.[21] Irrespective of the technicalities associated with police practices surrounding stop-and-search, the relationship between the police and black Britons continues to be somewhat strained. This is reflected by the grim reality that more than 5 per cent of black Britons view the use of force against a police officer as an acceptable form of political protest.

The long-lasting legacy of cases such as the Metropolitan Police's undercover investigation into the family of Stephen Lawrence following his racist murder in 1993 or the police-custody death of former British paratrooper Christopher Alder in 1998 continues to be problematic on this front. The Met, in particular, is in need of root-and-branch reform. Some may even argue that it should be disbanded and broken up into smaller, dynamic, effective police forces which are more responsive to local needs and concerns. Another option would be the absorption of London's outer boroughs into neighbouring police forces such as Essex, Hertfordshire, Kent, Surrey, and Thames Valley. Baroness Casey – who can hardly be considered 'woke' when one considers her hard-hitting work on matters of social integration – concluded in a report published in March 2023 that the Met's misconduct system had evidence of 'racial disparity'.[22] Testimonies from black, Asian and mixed-ethnic officers included concerns that raising racism-related issues (and other forms of discrimination) often led to being labelled as a 'troublemaker' – in some cases to unfair disciplinary action. One case study involved a serving police officer who had six misconduct cases raised against him, including oppressive conduct and harassment, neglect of duty and discriminatory behaviour linked to race and faith. Police forces need to engage better with civic associations and community organisations in a multi-agency effort to create well-trusted neighbourhood policing plans which strengthen both public security and respect for authority. This is especially relevant not only for London, but for other police forces that cover notable inner-city black-British populations, such as Greater Manchester, West Midlands, West Yorkshire and Avon and Somerset.

Stop-and-search has long been among the most controversial police practices in Britain. The government's crime-reduction strategy includes the relaxation of the current restrictions on police, with the aim of fighting rising knife crime. But critics have long argued that stop-and-search is racist. The *New Statesman*, for instance, in an article from July 2021 headlined 'How police stop and search remains racially biased', featured a chart showing stop-and-search rates by ethnicity.[23] It demonstrated that black Britons are the most likely ethnic group to be stopped and searched by the police – at a rate of 54 per 1,000 people. This is comfortably higher than the figure for British people of South Asian origin (17 per 1,000 people). Black people are 11 times more likely to be stopped and searched than white Brits (five per 1,000 people). Similarly, human-rights organisation Liberty argues that stop-and-search 'marginalises minority communities, destroys their relationships with the police, and funnels young people into the criminal-justice system'.[24]

But the assertion that stop-and-search is racially discriminatory is a classic example of the 'disparities = discrimination' paradigm that has come to define the left's understanding of racism. All other factors that might feed into disparate outcomes are ignored. Stop-and-search is primarily aimed at deterring knife-related offences in deprived inner-city neighbourhoods. You cannot explain these figures without looking at the demographic factors that are strongly associated with these types of offences – such as age, ethnicity and gender. We must also consider where these crimes are taking place, and what the demographics are in those areas. This is a sensitive subject that needs a nuanced approach, not to be seen only through the prism of race.

At the individual level, gang membership is a major risk factor for serious violence such as knife crime. At the community level, risk factors include living in an urban area characterised by material deprivation. These problems are highly concentrated in London. ONS data from 2020 shows that, in 2019–20, the capital had the highest regional rate for police-recorded offences involving a knife or sharp instrument: 179 offences per 100,000 people, compared with an England and Wales average of 82 offences per 100,000 people.[25] A 2019 BBC investigation found that 16 of the 20 most dangerous places in England and Wales for serious knife-crime offences are in London.[26] A government report found that, in 2017, 53 per cent of possession-of-knife suspects in London were black – and 37 per cent were black males under the age of 25.[27]

A press release produced by the London Assembly in February 2022 pointed out that, despite representing only 13 per cent of the capital's population, black Londoners account for 45 per cent of London's knife-murder victims, 61 per cent of knife-murder perpetrators and 53 per cent of knife-crime perpetrators in general.[28] This means that black Londoners are significantly more likely to be both victims and perpetrators of knife crime. To ignore these details when discussing disparities in stop-and-search rates makes little sense. Police measures which are designed to combat knife crime in London may be disproportionately used against young black men – but they also have the potential to save a disproportionate number of young black male lives.

But what about the charge that stop-and-search is pitting Britain's ethnic minorities against the police? While feelings of racial unfairness are held in the black-British mainstream over policing, the most recent Crime Survey for England and Wales undermines racially loaded 'police v. community' narratives. The survey shows that around two in three black people have confidence in their local police – not much lower than the corresponding figure of 74 per cent for white Brits. In fact, it shows that a number of non-white groups are more likely to have confidence in their local police than white Brits – namely, people of Bangladeshi, Indian and Chinese origin.[29] As stated in Chapter 1, according to a study by anti-racism advocacy group Hope Not Hate, 64 per cent of Britons from an ethnic-minority background agreed that the police were a force for good on the whole, and that any problems over racism were down to a small number of individuals.[30]

This is not to say that much more cannot be done to improve police–community relations – especially in deprived and ethnically diverse parts of the country. The recent Sewell report suggested that the legitimacy and accountability of police performing stop-and-search could be enhanced through body-worn video (BWV) cameras, for instance.[31] Police forces in Britain could also work closely with civic and community associations to foster public support for robust policing practices. The police certainly have a lot to do to earn or retain the trust of black Britons. But, at the same time, we must guard against the outright vilification of the police and the justice system. The framing of disparities in stop-and-search as a direct by-product of racial discrimination is not only crudely simplistic, but also threatens to undermine British race relations. The dismissal of stop-and-search as racist is yet another example of how the modern left is more interested in indulging in racial-grievance politics than in finding practical and inclusive ways to cultivate stronger ties between citizens and the institutions that are supposed to serve them.

The reality is that while some – quite reasonably – feel that more can be done to cultivate healthier police–community relations, the vast majority of ethnic-minority Britons have confidence in their local police force when it comes to the bread and butter of keeping communities safe. While it may be an inconvenience for fully fledged members of the grievance industry – such as Liberty – the majority reject the view that British police are plagued by 'systemic racism'. Concerns in black-British communities over perceived racial unfairness should be taken seriously, but we should not allow pessimistic identitarians to seize the narrative over policing in British democracy. A comfortable majority of black Britons maintain confidence in their local police forces, and have very little time for the radical 'defund the police' objectives associated with the radical elements of the BLM movement. On issues of policing, Britain's traditional ethnic minorities are not 'ACAB' ('all cops are bastards') types – the data tells us that they are generally constructive and optimistic citizens who are poorly represented by identitarian politicians and social activists who are ultimately focused on vilifying law enforcement and Britain at large.

Britain can do more to foster a merit-driven allocation of rewards and to tackle forms of political disaffection and institutional distrust in certain ethnic-minority communities – especially among British-born people of black-Caribbean origin who have seen their elders caught up in the *Windrush* scandal and understandably hold the view that the Met has not truly learnt from the grave mistakes it made in the days of Stephen Lawrence's racially motivated murder. Being an optimistic patriot who wants Britain to be the ultimate gold-standard example of a successful multiracial democracy, I believe that there is no room for complacency. Diversity brings its challenges, and addressing them takes considerable cooperation and willpower. We cannot afford to be self-satisfied or smug – a charge I would level at the 'denialists'.

Equally, the 'obsessives' are wrong about British democracy – the assertion that all of its systems are deliberately rigged against ethnic minorities is as baseless as it is divisive. I would agree with one of the key points made in the landmark Sewell report: there is a salience and attention to racial equality here in the UK – in policy-making, the media and academia – which is seldom found in Continental nations. In France, for instance, the collection of data based on race and ethnicity is deemed to be culturally unacceptable under its rigid model of fiercely secular universalism. And its traditionally puritanical commitment to defending the 'indivisible Republic' means that it has a socio-political reluctance to engage with matters of racism and discrimination faced by minorities – especially when it comes to Muslim communities originating from northern and western Africa. For all its flaws, Britain has established itself as a European leader in fostering social cohesion and economic fairness – especially when it comes to race, ethnicity and religion.

At the time of writing, we all live in a white-majority society with an established church – but one that also has a Hindu prime minister of Punjabi descent who was born in Southampton to African-born parents (although, based on the degree of political turmoil in recent times, this may not be the case once this book is published!). Some on the left responded to Rishi Sunak becoming our first non-white prime minister – and the first ethnic-minority holder of the office since Benjamin Disraeli, who played an integral role in the creation of the modern Conservative Party – by hurling divisive terms such as 'racial gatekeeper'. Labour backbencher Nadia Whittome said that Sunak becoming the head of the UK government was not 'a win for Asian representation' – a couched way of questioning his 'racial authenticity' on the grounds of his educational background and wealth.[32] These sentiments were echoed by Labour parliamentary candidate Faiza Shaheen, who urged her Twitter followers not to greet Sunak's likely victory as a triumph for diversity or social mobility on the basis that he is 'very rich' and 'went to [a] top private school'.[33] In a similar vein, Rupa Huq, Labour MP for Ealing Central and Acton since 2015, referred to the former chancellor, the Ghanaian-heritage Kwasi Kwarteng, as 'superficially black' due to his prestigious educational background and speaking style.[34] This is student-style amateurism that does not belong in a mature social-democratic political party.

There are elements of Sunak's life story that are somewhat questionable, such as his holding of a US green card. He also faced scrutiny when it was revealed that his wife, Akshata Murty, was not liable for UK taxes on her overseas earnings due to her non-domicile status. Being from Luton, I was not amused by a clip which emerged from the Tory leadership contest of July–September 2022 (won by Liz Truss) in which Sunak bragged to party members in the leafy, affluent town of Royal Tunbridge Wells that he had reorganised government formulas to redistribute funds away from supposedly 'overfunded' urban deprived areas.[35] And another video of Sunak in his younger years stumbling on the point of whether or not he had 'working-class friends' certainly doesn't portray him in the best light.[36]

But Sunak's rise to become prime minister of the UK cemented post-Brexit Britain's status as a relatively advanced multiracial democracy: a generally fair and tolerant society at ease with demographic diversity. In a 2020 poll carried out by Number Cruncher Politics, 84 per cent of white voters said either that they weren't bothered about the possibility of having a non-white prime minister in the future or that they would view it as a positive development.[37] While 32 per cent explicitly believed that it would be a positive development to be welcomed, just over half of white Brits said the ethnicity of the UK's prime minister was an irrelevance. Just 9 per cent thought that having a non-white prime minister would be a negative development – a fringe position that was needlessly amplified by race-obsessed grievance-manufacturers both at home and abroad. There was no racial backlash when Sunak arrived at Number Ten, contrary to what South African 'comedian' Trevor Noah suggested: the vast majority of British people either welcomed it as a positive political development or acknowledged it as a historic moment, but are ultimately focused on matters of policy substance and the quality of governance. This demonstrates the significant strides Britain has made as a modern multiracial democracy.

Irrespective of one's political persuasion and the more dubious elements of Sunak's background, his ascent to the premiership embodies a remarkable story of migrant-origin progress in a largely tolerant multiracial democracy – and that should be celebrated. He is an impressive example of social integration, hard work and socio-economic advancement. Born in Hampshire to immigrant parents (his father was a GP and his mother ran a local pharmacy), Sunak attended Winchester College, an independent boys' school, where he was head boy. He graduated with first-class honours from Lincoln College, Oxford. He went on to gain an MBA from Stanford University in California, winning a Fulbright scholarship. After working in the financial sector, he was elected to Parliament in May 2015, rising to the position of Chancellor of the Exchequer in February 2020, before becoming prime minister in October 2022.

The reality is that Sunak has an uplifting personal story to tell based on parental migrant aspiration, strong family values, academic excellence and professional advancement. The modern British left must strive to appeal to aspirational and advancing ethnic-minority communities across the country who, with a traditional emphasis on self-discipline, resilience, determination and optimism, reject the politics of grievance and increasingly represent an integral part of Britain's economic, social and cultural spheres of life. Indeed, there are ethnic-minority success stories based on robust intergenerational structures, a strong educational ethos and an unshakeable belief in social mobility throughout Britain. The left cannot be centred on grievance and victimhood – it must be a positive representative force for ethnic-minority communities who are appreciative of the opportunities, protections and freedoms provided under British democracy. Those aspirational, high-achieving and entrepreneurial non-white families in Britain must not be overlooked by the left in the name of protecting its treasured but ultimately toxic 'white-privilege' theories – their impressive levels of educational and socio-economic achievement set an example for many others in our society.

7

ETHNIC-MINORITY ACADEMIC AND PROFESSIONAL ADVANCEMENT

Some on the modern 'progressive' left offer the view that Britain is a fundamentally racist society in which the social, economic and political systems are deliberately rigged against ethnic minorities. It is true that our society is by no means perfect when it comes to equality of opportunity. In Chapter 1, I referred to jobs-based discrimination faced by those with 'culturally distant' names. There remains something of an unfavourable mismatch between academic qualifications and employment outcomes for ethnic minorities at large. Indeed, this was acknowledged by the 'controversial' Sewell report published by CRED in March 2021, which was far more balanced than some think. If jobs-based discrimination was addressed in a more robust manner, I suspect there would be even more ethnic-minority Brits in the professional and managerial classes. But, all too often, much of the British left goes overboard in its damning analysis of Britain's record on matters of fairness and opportunity – providing grossly inaccurate caricatures which ignore deeply encouraging forms of ethnic-minority success and advancement over the last few decades.

It is no secret that one of the spheres of British life where most ethnic-minority groups excel is education. When it comes to school attainment, many ethnic-minority pupils are steaming ahead of their peers in the white-British mainstream – especially white working-class boys who live in materially deprived and socially atomised post-industrial communities. While the UK branch of the BLM movement has – bizarrely – called for the 'decriminalisation' of black students in Britain's classrooms, pupils of black-African origin are now one of the highest-performing ethnic categories in terms of school attainment in England.[1] And when it comes to earnings, non-white workers of Chinese and Indian origin earn more than their white-British counterparts in the UK (in terms of median hourly pay).[2] Such data certainly exposes the lunacy which has contaminated our race-relations conversation – in which modern-day 'anti-racists' cosplaying as civil-rights activists from the era of American segregation try to kid others that we live in a white-supremacist society.

In this context, British Indians – admittedly diverse in terms of ethnic background, religious affiliation and migratory history – are a fascinating case study. The initial wave of Indian migration began in the 1950s, with a number of highly educated individuals from the western-Indian state of Gujarat coming to Britain to work as medical professionals in the NHS. There were also considerable inflows of Sikhs from Punjab – many of whom had been displaced following the 1947 partition and allocated low-quality land in what remained of Indian Punjab. Many of the first Indian migrants had personal links with the British military – particularly those from Punjab. For many of those who dutifully served in the British Indian Army and the Merchant Navy, relocating to Britain was less like moving to a foreign country than starting a new life in the 'motherland' of the Empire. This 'pre-arrival' emotional attachment and sense of pride meant that post-Second World War Britain essentially received patriotic servicemen who were born and raised in lands afar.

The story of Indian migration to Britain is, however, more complicated than the traditional 'origin–destination' flows which usually characterise migratory patterns. There was an earlier Indian diaspora to other parts of the British Empire – particularly East Africa, where a substantial number of Indians had been actively recruited by the UK government to work as administrative clerks and lower-level civil officials. These East African Indians were described as 'the filling' in the 'colonial sandwich', holding positions below that of the dominant British colonialists but above that of the subordinate African population. A large proportion of these migrants also established successful businesses, which eventually formed the backbone of East African economies.

When the East African countries gained independence from Britain in the 1960s, a number – in particular Uganda – introduced policies of 'Africanisation'. Under Idi Amin, in August 1972 the Ugandan government ordered those of Indian origin to leave the country within 90 days. As a thriving commercial and industrial class, the expelled Indian-origin population was, according to historian A. B. K. Kasozi, 'the grease that lubricated the upper sector of Uganda's economy'.[3] Their businesses were expropriated and transferred to Amin's cronies and sycophants, who simply did not have the skills or expertise to successfully run such enterprises. As well as being a fundamentally racist endeavour, Uganda's project of Africanisation was hugely counterproductive in terms of nation-state economic interest. Despite Britain introducing legislation in 1962 and 1968 to restrict entry rights for 'New Commonwealth' citizens, many East African Indians were eventually, in 1972, allowed to enter the country by Edward Heath's Conservative government. Like the East African Indians who decided to re-establish themselves in North America, those who were allowed to resettle in the UK have made notable economic contributions through their business acumen and entrepreneurial spirit.

British Indians represent one of the highest-performing ethnic groups in the UK, as they generally have stable family structures with a strong pro-education ethos, the vital foundations for personal development and socio-economic progress. While adopting a positive approach to social integration, British Indians have largely maintained durable internal structures, especially when it comes to family, faith and community. Rates of intra-ethnic marriage remain relatively high among this demographic, with civic associations and places of worship underpinning high-trust local communities. While it is important to recognise the degree of diversity among Britain's Indian diaspora, it is ultimately a collective success story – and this pattern of higher-than-mainstream levels of academic achievement and economic prosperity is replicated in Indian-origin communities across the Anglosphere. Indeed, Indian-origin households (which tend to be highly educated) have the highest median income out of all ancestries in the United States (with households of Taiwanese heritage also ranking highly).

There are a number of statistics that provide an insight into British Indian stability, resilience and success. Conforming to patterns found in other major liberal democracies such as the United States, British Indian children are the least likely to belong to a lone-parent household – only 6 per cent do so, according to the ONS.[4] By comparison, this figure rises to 19 per cent for their white-British peers, 43 per cent for children of black-African origin, and all the way to 63 per cent for dependants of black-Caribbean heritage. For the academic year 2020–21, Indian-heritage pupils had one of the highest 'Attainment 8' scores in England – 62.0 (out of 90), comfortably higher than the national average of 50.9 (the white-British mainstream registers 50.2).[5] A reflection of the education-oriented ethos and emphasis on self-discipline in well-ordered households, the temporary exclusion rate for Indian-origin pupils in England for 2018–19 was only 0.9 per cent.[6] This rose to 3.1, 6.0 and 10.7 per cent for Pakistani-, white-British- and black-Caribbean-origin pupils, respectively. The only ethnic group with a lower temporary exclusion rate for that academic year were pupils of Chinese origin (0.6 per cent).

There is no denying that the first generation of new-comers paved the way for current-day British Indian success, passing their dedicated work ethic, educational ethos, expert knowledge and business acumen down the generations. Here is a story of migrants, refugees and their descendants making notable contributions to British public life – in business, politics, media, entertainment, sport, and more. The fact that British Indians have been so successful and integrated into society should be celebrated by the left, whose identitarian contingent is much more interested in keeping ethnic minorities locked into a perpetual state of victimhood. The values of personal responsibility, individual initiative and self-sufficiency, which run deep in British Indian communities, challenge the left's grievance-fuelling narrative that Britain is a hotbed of systemic racism and structural discrimination.

The case study of British Indian success is reflected in the Sewell report, which offers an account of why there are variations between ethnic groups when it comes to academic achievement and socio-economic success.

While it may be unfashionable to say so, and though institutions in both the public and private sectors could do more to root out racial discrimination, we must not shy away from the reality that family dynamics and internal cultural attitudes can have a very real impact on the life trajectory of people living in Britain's competitive society. It is time for the debate on racial and ethnic inequalities in the UK to be guided by the realities on the ground – not what makes for fashionable coffee-table chatter.

If truth be told, I have looked with unease over the modern British left's relationship with successful British Indian families, which are gold-standard examples of quietly traditional values driving socio-economic progress. Indeed, Dr Samir Shah, who served on CRED, has argued that the advancement of many British Indian families – a notable number having moved from the traditionally Labour-voting inner cities into more Tory-leaning suburban areas – is 'troubling' for some.[7] Modern left-wing politics strongly emphasises racial equality and social justice – and, in principle, these are not necessarily bad things at all (in moderation, of course). The problem occurs when elements of the 'progressive left' are over-zealous in providing their 'allyship' to ethnic minorities who do not necessarily need or want it. Many British Indians do have a strong sense of fairness – but they are 'natural conservatives' who, in the words of Tory grandee Norman Tebbit, have 'a strong commitment to family values' and a 'resolute work ethic', as well as being 'keen on education, entrepreneurial and business-minded'.[8] While some sections of the identitarian left would love nothing more than to psychologically imprison all of Britain's ethnic and racial minorities in a hopeless state of grievance and victimhood, theirs is a toxic, anti-aspirational politics that would put off many upwardly mobile British Indian families in cities such as London, Birmingham, Wolverhampton and Coventry, as well as towns such as Slough and Bolton.

As discussed in Chapter 6, we have – at the time of writing – a British Indian family in 10 Downing Street. While much has been made of Rishi Sunak's non-white Asian identity, less has been said about his faith. The latest census data showed that there are now a million Hindus living in England and Wales – 1.7 per cent of the population.[9] When elected as MP for the constituency of Richmond in North Yorkshire in 2015, Sunak swore allegiance on the Bhagavad Gita, one of Hinduism's most sacred texts. He is most certainly a man of faith, which is most refreshing in an increasingly secular age. As Shah explains, in Hinduism, education is an important means to achieve the four primary aims of life: *dharma* (duty), *artha* (wealth), *kama* (pleasure) and *moksha* (liberation).[10] Education – especially in British Indian Hindu families – is widely seen as the most effective route towards providing for loved ones, creating wealth, living a satisfying life and reaching a position of economic freedom and independence. Indeed, Sunak himself has said that 'a good education is the closest thing we have to a silver bullet when it comes to making people's lives better'.[11]

Education is the absolute driving force for British Indian families. The statistics speak for themselves: a recent Institute for Fiscal Studies (IFS) report stated that 'over 50 per cent of Indians... have tertiary [degree-level or equivalent] qualifications, compared with 26 per cent of the white majority'.[12] The vast majority of British Indian families – the plurality being Hindus – have no time for any kind of mental slavery. Their central ideas – inspired by religious and cultural beliefs – are rooted in family values, hard work, education and prosperity. Instead of being troubled by successful and aspirational ethno-religious minorities and looking at their existence as an inconvenience to their social-justice narratives, the modern left should realise that these groups set an example for the rest of society, celebrate such forms of progress and be honest about the cultural and attitudinal factors which underpin social mobility in modern-day Britain.

While British Indians – especially East Africans who fled Africanisation in countries such as Uganda and Kenya – have established themselves as an inspirational national success story, there is a much smaller Asian ethnic-minority group worthy of special mention: the British Chinese. This section of the population – primarily of Han ancestry – constitutes the second-largest group of overseas Chinese-origin people in Western Europe (the largest being in France). The first waves of immigrants came between 1842 (the end of the First Opium War) and the 1940s, largely through treaty ports opened as concessions to the British after the Opium

Wars (such as Canton, Tianjin and Shanghai). Along with London, Chinese immigrants tended to settle in British port cities such as Liverpool and Cardiff. While there have been more recent streams of Chinese migrants from mainland China since the 1980s, a good number of British Chinese people in fact originate from other former British colonies, such as Canada, Australia, New Zealand, Singapore, Malaysia, Hong Kong and Mauritius. There are now established Chinese-origin communities in a string of other cities, including Manchester, Birmingham, Glasgow, Edinburgh and Belfast.

Compared to other ethnic minorities, British Chinese people are more geographically widespread and decentralised. With a proven track record of high academic and socio-economic achievement, the British Chinese community has been hailed as a socio-economic success story by a plethora of domestic sociologists. But what are the socio-cultural factors that help to produce such impressive educational and socio-economic outcomes among this population?

From my experience of the Chinese-origin population in my home town of Luton, I know that it places an exceptionally high value on education (including post-secondary academic attainment). This includes the provision of supplementary tutoring (irrespective of financial barriers, which have clearly reduced over time). Furthermore, as well as a cultural emphasis on effort and determination over innate ability, there tends to be robust parental intervention to reduce children's exposure to counterproductive influences (based on the 'Confucian paradigm of man'). An unshakeable belief in social mobility and advancement is another important part of the picture – hope over grievance; psychological freedom over mental slavery. As a demonstration of the cultural determination and resilience which characterise Britain's Chinese-origin communities, the 2020–21 average 'Attainment 8' score for Chinese-heritage pupils in England receiving special education needs (SEN) support was 55.8 – higher than the corresponding figure for the entire pupil population with no identified special educational needs (54.5).[13] This is a quite extraordinary outcome which reflects the cultural robustness at the very core of our Chinese-origin communities.

In this sense, there is a strong overlap between Britain's Indian-origin and Chinese-heritage populations when it comes to family characteristics and cultural dynamics – well-ordered family units where high educational attainment is often viewed as the most reliable route towards long-term economic security and financial self-sufficiency. At the heart of this is parental assertiveness and young people's respectfulness towards elders, factors which are bizarrely being interpreted by the modern left's more immature elements as 'hierarchical', 'oppressive' and restrictive of 'freedom' and 'creativity'. While much of the left may consider such arrangements to be 'old-fashioned', and support for traditional family units as a form of reactionary politics, their positive role in young people's educational performance and socio-economic progress cannot be underestimated. A degree of parental control and family-administered discipline is needed to set the next generation on the right path of progress and development.

In line with social and economic patterns in other Anglophone nations such as the United States, Canada and Australia, Britain's Indian and Chinese minorities are two successful and well-integrated ethnic groups that are setting the standards for others to follow. That aspirational, hard-working, driven families of migrant stock increasingly play a positive role in the social, economic and cultural life of the UK and other Western countries is an uplifting story that should be celebrated by the left. Surely progressive-liberal parties who believe that 'diversity is our strength' and that immigration is largely beneficial for host societies would champion such forms of ethnic-minority advancement? But I cannot help but feel that there is a growing discomfort over cases of success within British ethnic minorities – especially the country's upwardly mobile Indian-origin and Chinese-heritage minorities. This unease with non-white families being independent, entrepreneurial and self-sufficient is not felt by rabid right-wingers, however. The guilty tribes are progressive-liberal activists and hard-left 'anti-racists', for whom the existence of flourishing and resilient ethnic-minority communities is frustratingly at odds with their 'white privilege' theories and narratives about a 'systemically racist Britain'.

One might be forgiven for thinking that the left-leaning brigades of British political society are increasingly 'anti-minority' – especially when it comes to what is known as the 'soft bigotry of low expectations'. An illustration of this phenomenon concerns the high-performing Michaela Community School in north-west London, previously discussed in Chapter 1, at which some liberal-leftists have taken aim. Founded by leading educationalist Katharine Birbalsingh, the Wembley-based institution has the motto 'Work hard, be kind' – which, bizarrely, some have interpreted as potentially encouraging 'black and global majority pupils' to be 'compliant and subservient'.[14] The author of these words, journalist Sian Griffiths, sought to support her view by making the point that similar school mottos have been retired in the United States – the chief exporter of divisive identitarian initiatives – on such grounds. This is a classic case of US-inspired racial identity politics being imported into the UK by the mainstream liberal media classes, who are not truly interested in engaging with the traditional education-oriented ethos which runs deep in many of Britain's ethnic-minority communities.

The preference here is for young 'black and global majority' people (a substitute umbrella term that will quite possibly gain popularity now that broadcasters have pledged to phase out the 'BAME' acronym from their coverage) to be locked in a rebellious and unruly mindset – up-and-coming social-justice warriors dedicated to shattering fictitious forms of systemic racism and structural discrimination. Take, for example, the UK branch of the BLM movement calling for the 'decriminalisation' of black pupils in the classroom, as referred to earlier in this chapter. But ethnic-minority pupils who embrace a dedicated work ethic and are committed to making the most of educational opportunities in order to progress in life are not much use to the grievance-manufacturing industry. In fact, black pupils' outperforming their white-British peers at school and having reduced levels of exclusion are the worst possible outcomes for the grievance lobby, which is intent on portraying the British education sector as systemically racist. And the framing of traits such as self-discipline and well-ordered behaviour as 'white characteristics' is deeply insulting to traditional ethnic-minority families, who firmly believe in the value of adopting a regimented and disciplined approach to educational advancement, something that lays the foundations of longer-term economic security.

Indeed, encouraging educational excellence among more 'recently arrived' ethnic groupings should help to improve levels of economic self-reliance in relatively deprived communities. The child-poverty rate in the British Bangladeshi population is higher than any other ethnic group: 61 per cent.[15] This is down to myriad migratory, geographical, social and cultural factors. For example, most British Bangladeshis originate from deprived rural villages in Sylhet, with half of the population living in high-cost London. Furthermore, a disproportionate number of men are concentrated in low-paid transportation and hospitality roles, while conservative gender norms mean that there is a relatively high level of female economic inactivity. To put the British Bangladeshi child-poverty figure into perspective, the corresponding figure for the British Chinese population is 12 per cent (notably lower than the white mainstream rate of 26 per cent).[16] However, a culture in which academic excellence is promoted in households containing two parents – who encourage their children to take advantage of the educational opportunities they never had – is allowing British Bangladeshis to reap rewards. Recent 'Attainment 8' scores in England show that pupils of Bangladeshi origin are outperforming the white-British mainstream, with average scores of 55.6 and 50.2 out of 90, respectively.[17]

For certain ethnic-minority groups who are residentially concentrated in a particular part of the country, improvements in institutional standards across a select number of schools can go a long way. Over the last two decades, there has been a serious jump in the level of school attainment among England-based pupils of Bangladeshi origin. Heavily concentrated in east London, much of this can be attributed to improvements in teaching quality across a string of schools in boroughs such as Tower Hamlets. Key interventions have included the state-funded 'London Challenge' scheme and sharpened forms of school governance fostered by the government's academies programme. In addition, the 'Teach First' programme has provided a diverse pool of talented and idealistic new teachers to schools serving disadvantaged communities in traditionally poorer London boroughs. This has been transformative for Bangladeshi-heritage pupils in east London, who, compared with their white-British peers, have the added advantage of being relatively well situated in traditional family-oriented social structures with a strong emphasis on education.

Pupils of black-African origin – including a notable section of young people belonging to families who have fled civil unrest and political persecution – also have a higher 'Attainment 8' score than the white-British mainstream: 52.2 out of 90.[18] This is also 8.2 points higher than the average for black-Caribbean-heritage pupils (44.0 out of 90).[19] In this case, black-African-origin pupils are performing better than the white-British mainstream, while their co-racial peers of Caribbean heritage are performing notably worse on average. Similar patterns emerge when it comes to rates of school exclusion in England. For the school year of 2018–19, the temporary exclusion rate for black-African-origin pupils was lower than the white-British mainstream (4.1 and 6.0 per cent, respectively). Meanwhile, more than one in ten pupils of black-Caribbean heritage – 10.7 per cent – received a fixed-period exclusion. The pattern is replicated for permanent exclusions – black African: 0.07 per cent; white British: 0.1 per cent; black Caribbean: 0.25 per cent.[20]

The level of school attainment and rates of exclusion within England's broader black-pupil population perhaps provide some insight into why the grievance-manufacturing industry insists on using crudely homogenising terms such as 'black community' when peddling their narratives of victimhood. If you merge all the relevant ethnic groups into overarching 'white' and 'black' categories, the former has a marginally higher average 'Attainment 8' score (50.2 and 50.0 out of 90, respectively), and a marginally lower permanent exclusion rate (0.1 per cent and 0.11 per cent, respectively).[21] By blending racial categories, important ethnic differences in educational outcomes between co-racial groups – such as pupils of black-African and black-Caribbean heritage – are concealed. It is far easier to paint the education system as having a serious racism problem with these broader figures based on racial identity, and significantly harder to do this when one considers the fact that England's pupils of black-African origin have higher levels of school attainment and lower levels of exclusion than their white-British counterparts. In this context, the term 'black' masks better-than-white-British outcomes for the black-African-origin population and worse-than-white-British outcomes for the black-Caribbean-heritage population.

The modern British left should not be in the business of downplaying or concealing ethnic-minority success on the grounds that to champion it would run the risk of undermining their pseudo-intellectual white-privilege theories. Doing so gives the impression that the left is reluctant to celebrate forms of ethnic-minority excellence and to appreciate the fact that these achievements are often underpinned by robust family units and traditional values such as self-discipline. Entertaining flimsy ideas of 'racial privilege' also threatens to make the Labour

Party look like an unrelatable political organisation which is uncaring towards educational underachievement and socio-economic stagnation in white-British communities. This is far from ideal if the party has genuine aspirations to restore its status as the leading political force in left-behind, racially homogeneous 'Red Wall' constituencies in the provincial Midlands and northern England.

In various spheres of life – politics, business, health-care, education, media, entertainment, sports, and others – many of Britain's ethnic-minority traditionalists are making a genuine success of themselves. More work must be done to improve equality of opportunity in our country – especially when it comes to fighting jobs-based discrimination. But we should take pride in the fact that we have both an ethnically and religiously diverse society in which more ethnic-minority people are slowly but surely reaching positions of power and influence as a result of the specialist knowledge and professional exper-tise which has been developed through their dedicated work ethic. There is some way to go if we are to become a truly meritocratic society, but the diversification of the professional and managerial classes shows that progress is being made. The glass ceiling has not quite been shat-tered, but notable breakthroughs have taken place over the course of the twenty-first century.

While a number of Western countries lag behind Britain in terms of ethnic-minority participation in par-liamentary politics, the occupation of the great offices of state by non-white politicians has been normalised in our democracy. Irrespective of one's political leanings and party affiliation, that is a victory for multiracial Britain. Sons and daughters of first-generation migrants – some of whom came to Britain with few socio-economic resources – are now at the heart of national decision-making processes. Of course, these decisions should always be scrutinised by wider civil society in terms of their social and economic impact (especially on the most deprived households in Britain), but the political advancement of British ethnic minorities is a victory for integration in our country. One can disagree with the policy positions held by former Tory leadership candidates such as Suella Braverman and Kemi Badenoch, but still appreciate the degree of progress made by non-white women in national politics – with other Western European democracies trailing Britain on this front.

Another non-white woman who has had quite an impact on Britain's socio-political landscape is the afore-mentioned leading educationalist Katharine Birbalsingh – the country's 'strictest headmistress'. Michaela Community School in Wembley, which she co-founded and leads, is one of our country's most successful educational hubs – indeed, in 2022, its value-added (progress) score at GCSE level was the highest for any school in England. With her thoroughly Commonwealth background, New Zealand-born and Canada-raised Birbalsingh, who is of Indo-Guyanese and Jamaican ancestry, embodies one of the finest migratory stories in modern Britain – a no-nonsense woman who helped set up and spearheads an exceptional educational institution in a relatively deprived and hyper-diverse part of north-west London.

While those of a liberal-left disposition attack her for opposing 'modern' teaching styles which they claim encourage individual 'creativity' and 'freedom', Birbalsingh's emphasis on small-*c* conservative values – hard work, self-discipline, resilience, duty, responsibility, service and honour – go down a treat with ethnic-minority tradition-alists (many of whom, the left should be reminded, live in traditionally Labour-voting parts of inner-city London). All those who are genuinely serious about young peo-ple's academic progress and wider personal development should engage in a positive manner with Birbalsingh's support for traditional methods – her track record for delivering results in multi-ethnic, working-class Britain speaks for itself.

Labour will not achieve electoral success by drawing inspiration from doom-and-gloom identitarians obsessed with America's bitterly polarising race politics – but by understanding what is working in Britain in terms of cultural values and social practice. The fact is that much of the mainstream can learn from the robust family bonds, intergenerational cohesion, strong educational ethos, entrepreneurial spirit and everyday optimism that char-acterise aspirational ethnic-minority communities across the country. As we have seen, on a range of educational and economic metrics, multiple ethnic groups – especially people of Chinese and Indian heritage – are now outper-forming the white-British mainstream. In some cases, ethnic-minority pupils from a materially disadvantaged background are achieving better exam results than their middle-class white peers – which means that the conversation has to be wider than the current focus on new-age 'racial justice' and broadened into matters of culture.

The left must not pigeonhole itself by constantly interpreting outcomes through the reductive prism of race. An obsession with racial identity obscures the enduring influence of class when it comes to rewards and opportunities. The Labour Party should shift more of its thinking on equality towards matters of deprivation, but it must not be an unbridled 'class-warrior' party either – there are instances of poorer ethnic-minority communities being able to compensate for poverty-related disadvantages through stable family dynamics, the pooling of community resources and thriving civic assets. While tackling socio-economic inequalities should be restored to the heart of Labour's thinking, the British left must also emphasise the social value of well-structured families, community pride and the wholesome sense of belonging provided by religious and cultural associations. This will help to win back and shore up its support among ethnic-minority traditionalists – some of whom have either shifted to the Tories or given them more of a hearing in recent times.

There are forms of social capital in many ethnic-minority communities that do not exist to the same extent in the white-British mainstream – especially 'hollowed-out', post-industrial and coastal communities defined by relatively high rates of family instability and limited civic assets for their young. If one looks into ethnic-minority communities in Labour-voting towns such as Luton or Slough, one will be hard pressed to find the politics of grievance and victimhood – it would be far easier to find hard-nosed but ultimately caring families who encourage their young to make the most of the opportunities offered to them. This support can extend beyond the family, often being provided by 'community elders'. These social structures and cultural dynamics cannot be ignored in national conversations on young people's academic progress and professional advancement in multi-ethnic Britain.

While fully fledged members of the grievance industry are either uncomfortable with acknowledging the existence of thriving and resilient ethnic-minority communities or see them as having overcome rampant forms of 'systemic racism', my view is rather different. Family-oriented and community-spirited minorities have rejected liberal anti-traditionalism and have taken advantage of opportunities offered by a country that – for all its flaws – boasts some of the most robust anti-discrimination protections and equality bodies in the world. Britain is a place with a reasonably functional state-funded education system and an advanced economy that promotes entre-preneurialism and ingenuity. By championing the academic excellence and socio-economic success which can be found in ethnic-minority communities across Britain, the left will be able to cultivate an inclusive and optimistic narrative that can appeal to many – a positive alternative to the demoralising BLM-inspired narrative.

I may well be accused by the grievance industry and race lobby of looking at modern Britain through rose-tinted spectacles, but I suspect that their depressingly gloomy perspectives and aggressively anti-system sentiments are not shared by many of the traditional, determined, hard-working families who make up Britain's rising ethnic-minority communities. If the British left thinks that the politics of pessimism is a winning one, then it should think again. The electorate will not trust a party that it believes is unable to see the best in Britain – especially on matters of fairness and equality.

Labour usually commands the support of an overwhelming majority of ethnic-minority voters – but it cannot take them for granted. This does not mean ramping up the mollycoddling identitarian rhetoric in which non-white people are all too often portrayed as helpless victims of racism in desperate need of 'allyship' and protection; it means fostering a fairer society where traditional ethnic minorities are better appreciated for the immense contributions they make to the economic, political, social and cultural spheres of British life. An ambitious and optimistic politics that wants Britain to be the standard-bearer for multiracial democracies in matters of equality of opportunity, social cohesion and national sense of belonging is what is needed. The country craves a new social and cultural settlement.

8

TOWARDS A RELEVANT
TRADITIONAL LEFT

The Labour Party has often been referred to as a 'broad church' – one that incorporates a supposedly 'rich' diversity of views and interests. But if that church becomes too broad, it can begin integrating radical and unrepresentative views which present a fundamentally warped view of British society and its institutions. This places a strain on social solidarity and ultimately undermines the credibility of the contemporary left. A mature social-democratic politics on the left should not draw inspiration from the American-inspired race politics as embodied by the BLM movement. Britain is not America – they are separate societies with vastly different histories and current-day circumstances when it comes to race relations, social cohesion and broader socio-political stability.

Presenting issues such as racial discrimination and police brutality as shared, transatlantic problems, as so-called 'anti-racists' increasingly do, is not reflective of the reality on the ground. The January 2021 ICM Unlimited poll showed that fewer than three in ten Brits (29 per cent) believe that the UK is a fundamentally racist society; more than double – 64 per cent – think the same about the United States.[1] When presented with the statement 'the UK does not have a problem with police brutality', around one in five Brits – 22 per cent – disagrees. This level of disagreement increases more than threefold to 67 per cent when it comes to the statement 'the US does not have a problem with police brutality'.[2] The sheer absurdity of British BLM protestors in London chanting 'Don't shoot' at police officers shows how the United States' law-enforcement issues have been brainlessly imported into the UK's so-called 'anti-racist' politics.

This is not to say that the British left should not hold the police to account on matters of discrimination. As we saw in Chapter 6, the findings of the March 2023 Casey report into the Metropolitan Police made for grim reading – including the discovery that hundreds of Met police officers have been getting away with breaking the law, with many claims of sexual misconduct, misogyny, racism and homophobia being poorly handled.[3] London needs a policing structure that is able to attract a diverse pool of courageous and decent individuals who are passionate about keeping its neighbourhoods as safe as possible. As it stands, it is failing miserably. It will be missing out on authentic on-the-ground intelligence that can boost the overall quality of its service. There needs to be a clearing out of the Augean stables. However, the British left should act as a bridge between the police and communities with low levels of institutional trust – adopting a constructive approach that heals wounds, not one that deepens them. After all, the majority of ethnic-minority Brits – including those of black-Caribbean origin – have confidence in their local police force to do the bread-and-butter work. This is ultimately about police forces gaining the respect of local communities and providing a secure environment for all of their workers – irrespective of race, ethnicity, religious belief, sex or sexual orientation.

The latest census data shows that we are becoming a more ethnically and religiously heterogeneous society. This will inevitably bring challenges when it comes to social cohesion and public confidence in the performance of institutions – both state and private. The public disorder largely between Muslim and Hindu youths in traditionally Labour-voting Leicester – a city usually considered a paragon of 'multiculturalism' – in August–September 2022 showed how social cohesion can unravel in seemingly peaceable parts of the country. Compared to other major industrialised democracies such as the United States, France and Germany, Britain has a relatively successful multi-ethnic, religiously diverse society – but we must not rest on our laurels. Integrating our diverse communities into a truly cohesive whole should be at the heart of an ambitious social agenda for the British left – one which strives for Britain to establish itself as the top-of-the-league example of an advanced diverse democracy in the modern world. Diversity is only a strength if it is tied together by shared values, mutual obligations and a sense of common purpose. According to an October 2022 poll by YouGov, nearly half of the British people – 46 per cent – believe that more needs to be done to strengthen relations between different ethnic and religious communities. This rose to 71 per cent for those who voted for Labour in the 2019 general election – voters who are relatively young, are more likely to live in diverse parts of 'Urban Britain' and ultimately have greater exposure to racial, ethnic and religious tensions.[4] A society defined by high levels of social trust and mutual understanding should be a dream for the British political left – it is these kinds of societies that are better able to compensate for market imperfections through the welfare state, and have lower levels of crime and higher rates of psychological well-being.

There is, however, one often-overlooked 'risk' to greater social integration: as people mix more with others of different racial, ethnic and religious backgrounds, they may be more likely to compare their life circumstances and experiences of institutions with those of a different demographic – and this could even include their spouse, extended family, step-relatives or close friends. This is precisely why a robust commitment to objectivity and impartiality should be at the heart of professional services provided by the state – whether it is the NHS or the police. This also means that the modern Labour Party needs to take a lead on how to foster a labour market which is based on the merit-based allocation of opportunities and rewards. Britain should strive to have a truly 'fair work' society – and that includes an anti-racist employment strategy that rejects US-style 'affirmative action' but ensures greater fairness through improvements in recruitment procedures, workplace participation and existing anti-discrimination regulation.

There will always be a moral imperative to ensuring that everyone in our society is treated fairly in the labour market. That should always be the first and most important consideration. But the left should not exclusively couch such an agenda in the moralising language of 'racial fairness' and 'social justice' – it should also frame this anti-racist employment strategy in terms of wealth creation and economic profit (which are anything but dirty phrases for ethnic-minority traditionalists who run successful private-sector enterprises up and down the country). Research has shown that companies in the top quartile for ethnic/cultural diversity on executive teams were notably more likely to have industry-leading profitability.[5] A more inclusive workforce makes sense from a societal and economic point of view. Indeed, a government-commissioned review carried out by Tory peer Ruby McGregor-Smith in 2017 found that the potential benefit to the UK economy from full representation of ethnic-minority individuals across the labour market, through improved participation and progression, was estimated to be £24 billion a year – which, at the time, represented 1.3 per cent of the UK's GDP.[6] Britain's anti-racist political movement must not be hijacked by hard-left, BLM-style pseudo-revolutionaries who wish to dismantle the market economy – the case for greater fairness in our diverse labour market is not simply a principled moral stance; it can also be justified from a wealth-creating perspective.

However, the contemporary British left cannot afford to view complex forms of social and economic disadvantage through the reductive prism of race – especially in a country which, for all its flaws, is a world-leading one when it comes to anti-discrimination protections for its racial minorities. Despite a lengthy period of Tory-led rule, Britain still lacks a social-policy agenda which has families at the heart of it. Indeed, much of the Conservative parliamentary party has been guilty of idolising Boris Johnson, a man with a spectacularly chaotic family and marital history and who has a somewhat questionable relationship with the concept of loyalty. It largely exists as a 'CINO' party – 'Conservative In Name Only'. There remains an influential tendency within the party that supports a certain free-market liberalism which prioritises the 'freedom' of the individual above all social obligations – which is perhaps not ideal when one considers that Britain is a global leader when it comes to family breakdown and crashing marriage rates.

Labour must be brave and courageous in talking about the social value of stable family structures and the positive impact of healthy marriages on young people's development. It should not be held hostage by politically correct activists who claim to be 'progressive' but refuse to acknowledge that secure families remain the finest spring-board when it comes to youth progression in the spheres of education and employment. The left must make use of its experienced politicians – especially those with quietly conservative lifestyles – and push the case for a 'social-justice traditionalism' that puts the family at the front and centre of debates on security and opportunity. This would resonate with 'family first' ethnic-minority traditionalists across the country – who are not necessarily guaranteed to provide their electoral support in perpetuity, by any stretch of the imagination. This is where the modern British left must be careful – especially when it comes to issues such as gender self-identification. The Labour Party must not risk alienating decent ethnic-minority tradition-alists through forms of radical cultural liberalism.

And this leads rather nicely into my next point – there is a progressive-activist tendency that has taken hold in the spheres of politics, education, media and entertain-ment that is responsible for peddling grossly inaccurate caricatures about the life of ethnic, racial and religious minorities living in Britain. The modern British left would do well to distance itself from American-inspired, BLM-style narratives on matters of race and equality. Unfortunately, there are far too many Labour politicians who are part of this grievance-manufacturing ecosystem – wilfully misrepresenting British ethnic minorities who are relatively satisfied and optimistic when compared with the white-British mainstream. The warped presentation of Britain as a racist hellhole whose economic and social systems are deliberately rigged is not only not rooted in reality, but threatens to turn away aspirational and advancing ethnic-minority families. These are voters who may believe that more needs to be done to strengthen equality of opportunity, but are still very much of the view that Britain is a land which presents its fair share of opportunities to thrive. The narrative-setting should not advance the alienating view that Britain is a fundamentally bigoted country that must self-flagellate over its record on race relations – rather, it should say this: 'Britain remains one of the most successful multiracial democracies on earth – how can we make it the global gold-standard example?' An aspirational Britain should be one that takes pride in the significant strides made over race relations but also one that guards against complacency and strives to improve.

The modern British left would do well to understand that some of the strongest patriotic sentiments can be found among its ethnic-minority communities. One of the greatest patriots I know is my own mother – born and raised in Bangladesh and resident in the UK since her early twenties, she has established herself as a dutiful British citizen who has made considerable social contributions in our home town of Luton. Through her professional expertise and dedicated work ethic, she has led efforts to set up from scratch grassroots community organisations – now thriving civic associations which provide important forms of social assistance as well as representing uplifting sources of cultural belonging. The left must not allow itself to become obsessed with racial and religious identity politics – rather, it needs to invest time and energy into championing place-based identities and appreciating civic forms of belonging. Discrimination – such as the unjust and prejudicial treatment of racial and religious minorities – is not to be tolerated. The risk for much of the left, however, is drowning in the pool of doom-and-gloom miserableness – losing sight of the deeply encouraging on-the-ground patriotism which exists in supposedly 'oppressed' and 'marginalised' groups. After all, the comfortable majority of black Brits attach importance to their British national identity – three in four British Muslims believe that Britain is a good place to live for their co-religionists.

The topic of the role of faith and religion is one that needs to be carefully managed by the Labour Party. All too often, it has sought to curry favour with particular ethno-religious minorities by picking sides when it comes to sectarian tensions and foreign territorial disputes – something that is not only electorally unsustainable but fundamentally undermines the British left's historic reputation for caring about social solidarity. The contemporary British left must stand with patriotic ethnic-minority traditionalists by tackling extreme religio-political ideologies in all shapes and forms – especially when it comes to the prevailing terror threat of Islamist extremism. Labour cannot afford to be squeamish over discussions about Islamist extremism – if it continues to be, it will be letting down plenty of anti-Islamist British Muslims who value the protections and freedoms ingrained in British liberal-democratic culture. Rather, the left should promote a shared cultural appreciation of faith – one based on family values and community spirit, celebrating the social value of places of worship and religious civic associations which provide a spiritual sense of belonging and rootedness. This would help Labour shore up its support in one of its most reliable electoral strongholds – the 'cosmopolitan' city of London, which is the most socially conservative region in the whole of the UK. This shared appreciation of faith can also bring together Kashmiri Muslims in Luton, Gujarati Hindus in Leicester, Punjabi Sikhs in Wolverhampton, Orthodox Jews in Bury, Goan Roman Catholics in Swindon, West African Protestants in Milton Keynes and Nepalese Buddhists in Aldershot.

Aldershot is home to a patriotic Nepalese Buddhist contingent – with some locals affectionately referring to their Hampshire town as 'Little Kathmandu'. These settled-in communities include Gurkhas with a decorated British Army background. It has been estimated that 3,300 Gurkhas – widely regarded as deeply courageous and highly skilled soldiers – currently serve in our military. There are 26 recipients of the Victoria Cross – the highest award for gallantry – from the Brigade of Gurkhas. The worst of the contemporary British left are fixated with 'decolonising' the school curriculum and portraying British history as one dominated by brutal conquest, slavery and genocide. Why not call for a greater educational emphasis on the contribution made by Asian, African and Caribbean servicepeople to Allied efforts in defeating fascism?

Indeed, Field Marshal Sir Claude Auchinleck, who served as commander-in-chief of the Indian Army during the Second World War, asserted that the British 'couldn't have come through both wars if they hadn't had the Indian Army'.[7] We as a country must recognise the immense courage and bravery shown by men who served in the British Indian Army – such as Subedar Khudadad Khan, VC. Born in Chakwal (now a city in modern-day Pakistan) in 1888, he was the first British Indian subject to be a recipient of the Victoria Cross. He was given this award for performing an act of bravery as a 26-year-old in battle at the Belgian village of Hollebeke in October 1914. During the Second World war, the King's African Rifles (KAR) was involved in military campaigns against Italian forces in East Africa, Japanese forces in Burma and the Vichy French in the 1942 Battle of Madagascar. One of the most moving images I came across during a recent VE Day anniversary was of two elderly gentlemen, Alford Gardner and Lionel Roper. As young men, both travelled from Jamaica to join the RAF during the Second World War. It is war heroes like these, born and raised in the Caribbean, to whom we owe a great deal. The modern British left is quite rightly open and expressive when it comes to showing its appreciation for the NHS – but it ought to do the same for the armed forces.

Another traditional institution which has increasingly come into the firing line of the identitarian British left is Buckingham Palace, which has also been vilified by the Sussexes, who have peddled grievance-fuelling narratives in a desperate attempt to boost their social status and financial security. The reality is that the royal family and some of its senior aides have contributed far more to community cohesion than many so-called 'anti-racists' ever could. The late Queen Elizabeth II's magnificent seven-decade reign was the rock that modern Britain was built on. Her Majesty was a champion of inter-religious dialogue and promoted ecumenism – reaching out to non-Protestant denominations in her role as Supreme Governor of the Church of England. This is especially relevant when one considers that one of the fastest-growing ethnic categories in our society is the 'White Other' group – which contains a notable number of Polish Catholics and orthodox Romanians. While critics might sneer at the monarchy, there is no doubt in my mind that Queen Elizabeth played an integral part in fostering what is now one of the better examples of an advanced multi-faith democracy in the modern world. In a quite moving revelation, the British Jewish *Times* columnist Daniel Finkelstein famously reported that his grandmother – a refugee from the now Ukrainian city of Lviv – once said: 'While the Queen is safe in Buckingham Palace, we're safe in Hendon Central.'[8]

Even after her passing, she remains a national symbol of unity and harmony. 'The Queue' for Her Majesty's lying-in-state brought together patriotic Brits from all walks of life, who connected with one another as they waited to pay their respects to the ultimate public servant. It was a wholesome demonstration of how traditional institutions and a ceremonial figurehead can be agents of social solidarity in a modern democracy. Her eldest child, King Charles III, has continued with his mother's 'progressive conservatism' – having referred to Britain as 'a community of communities' and himself as 'the defender of all faiths'. He is certainly a friend of many British Muslims – having spoken positively about the contributions of Muslims to the European Renaissance, the virtues of Islamic finance and Islam's approach to the environment. Mature social democrats in Britain would do well to ignore radical anti-monarchists and their pseudo-revolutionary games – and recognise that they have a strong cultural ally in Buckingham Palace.

It is time for the modern British left to better represent the values, beliefs and principles which characterise traditional-minded ethnic-minority communities across the country. While it should always be in the business of rooting out discrimination and tackling prejudicial treatment wherever it exists, it should not be consumed by the politics of grievance and victimhood which is being imported from the United States. It may be an inconvenience to those who believe that religion does more harm than good, view 'the family' as a unit of hierarchical oppression and think Britain has a fundamentally racist society – but the traditional triad of faith, family and flag is alive and well among our ethnic minorities. In many such communities, one will often find forms of educational success and socio-economic prosperity which represent uplifting family-oriented and community-spirited stories based on a strong work ethic, optimism, mental resilience, disciplined self-study and entrepreneurial skills. This is precisely why the left must offer more than pessimism – something which recognises the fine contributions and outstanding achievements made by Britain's ethnic minorities in various spheres of life.

At the time of writing, Labour intends to introduce a new Race Equality Act in the event of its returning to power. Supposedly experienced frontbench politicians should not insult the British people by presenting complex social and economic disparities through a reductive race-based lens – least of all, the country's ethnic-minority traditionalists, who understand the significance of family structure and community culture. Two of the biggest challenges for the country are improving social mobility in a stubbornly class-structured society and reducing regional inequality in one of the most inter-regionally imbalanced economies in the industrialised world. And, to be frank, for some communities, the main problems they face are not 'institutional racism' or 'systemic discrimination' – but instead fatherlessness, intergenerational disconnection and a fundamental lack of civic spirit. While the left should support practical steps to strengthen equality of opportunity, it must also be realistic about what the British state can achieve. It must also promote notions of personal responsibility, family duty and civic obligation. This is the kind of narrative-setting craved by many of

Britain's ethnic-minority communities – not the constant barrage of pseudo-intellectual identitarianism which threatens to put them off in high numbers.

The greatest shaper of life chances is not racial identity, ethnic origin or religious affiliation – it is one's family dynamics and the well-being of one's local neighbourhood (economic, social and cultural). Notions of 'white privilege' and 'racial oppression' look beyond farcical when one considers how young British people belonging to our Indian-, Chinese- and Nigerian-heritage communities are steaming ahead of their white-British peers in multiple spheres of life. It may be a controversial point to make, but perhaps elements of white working-class Britain could learn a thing or two from many of our aspirational and buoyant ethnic-minority communities, which are defined by family loyalty, high civic activity, a strong focus on education and a prideful relationship with their faith. A relevant left must recognise that Britain is a relatively successful multiracial democracy whose traditional ethnic minorities enjoy considerable regional freedoms – this should be celebrated. But it has to be a courageous socio-political force for good which aspires to a better Britain – one which brings our diverse communities closer through bonds of social trust, reciprocated respect and mutual understanding. Strengthening community cohesion should be at the heart of an ambitious social-policy agenda which aims for Britain to be the truest gold-standard example of an advanced and diverse industrialised democracy.

Cultivating social solidarity contributes towards the sustenance of the welfare state – something that all left-wing traditionalists should care about. The modern British left must do this by emphasising the values which unite many of us as people – the prioritisation of commonality over difference is needed more than ever. It can achieve this by championing the undeniable value of stable family structures, supporting a shared appreciation of faith and taking pride in Britain's cultural heritage and historical achievements. This effort should incorporate British people of all races, ethnicities and faiths – binding together our rich tapestry of peoples whose collective origins cover the whole world.

The modern British left should put aside the anti-aspirational politics which all too often frames traditional ethnic minorities as victims in desperate need of liberal 'allyship'. There are thriving ethnic-minority communities across our country which are the backbone of Britain – something that should be shouted from the rooftops. The vast majority of ethnic-minority Brits are not represented by tribal America-obsessed activists who secretly want preferential treatment on the grounds of race – they expect fairness, not favours. They do not want their public institutions to pander and succumb to unrepresentative group interests – but for them to be effective and responsive, to carry out their day-to-day activities in the spirit of impartiality, decency and propriety. And for the many, family, community, country and faith are all central to their being and sense of belonging. And it is time that their quietly traditional values, which provide solid grounding in their lives, were better appreciated by the British left of today.

This is how the contemporary British left can become a truly relevant force among patriotic, community-spirited, family-oriented ethnic minorities who are appreciative of the opportunities, freedoms and protections of British democracy. It is how they move beyond the politics of grievance.

Endnotes

1 'Sir Vince: Brexit voters driven by nostalgia for a "white" Britain', BBC News [website] (11 March 2018). Available at https://www.bbc.co.uk/news/av/uk-politics-43367293 (last accessed 18 January 2023).

2 Julia Ward, 'Still fighting for Europe for the many – join us for this mass demo against the right wing fascist coup that is Brexit' [Twitter post] (14 June 2019). Available at https://twitter.com/julie4north/status/1139650056158662657?s=20&t=AyQkZzsNftlq3ITx10vi_w (last accessed 24 February 2023).

3 Jessica Elgot, 'David Lammy says comparing ERG to Nazis "not strong enough"', *Guardian* (14 April 2019). Available at https://www.theguardian.com/politics/2019/apr/14/comparing-erg-to-nazis-not-strong-enough-says-david-lammy (last accessed 18 January 2023).

4 'EU referendum: local results: L', BBC News [website], available at https://www.bbc.co.uk/news/politics/eu_referendum/results/local/l (last accessed 23 January 2023).

5 Martin Rosenbaum, 'Local voting figures shed new light on EU referendum', BBC News [website] (6 February 2017). Available at https://www.bbc.co.uk/news/uk-politics-38762034 (last accessed 23 January 2023).

6 'EU referendum: local results: H', BBC News [website]. Available at https://www.bbc.co.uk/news/politics/eu_referendum/results/local/h (last accessed 23 January 2023); 'EU referendum: local results: S', BBC News [website]. Available at https://www.bbc.co.uk/news/politics/eu_referendum/results/local/s (last accessed 23 January 2023). 'EU referendum: local results: B', BBC News [website]. Available at https://www.bbc.co.uk/news/politics/eu_referendum/results/local/b (last accessed 23 January 2023).

7   Rakib Ehsan, 'Inside the British Asian Brexit vote – and why it contains a few surprises', UK in a Changing Europe [website] (18 February 2017). Available at https://ukandeu.ac.uk/inside-the-british-asian-brexit-vote-and-why-it-contains-a-few-surprises/ (last accessed 23 January 2023).

8   Laura Smith-Spark, Nima Elbagir and Barbara Arvanitidis, 'The greatest trick racism ever pulled was convincing England it doesn't exist', CNN [website] (22 June 2020). Available at https://edition.cnn.com/2020/06/22/europe/black-britain-systemic-racism-cnn-poll-gbr-intl/index.html?utm_content=2020-06-22T14%3A13%3A32&utm_source=twCNNi&utm_term=link&utm_medium=social (last accessed 18 January 2023).

9   Eliane Thoma-Stemmet, 'Systemic racism exists in the UK at every level of government and society', *Varsity* [website] (12 June 2020). Available at https://www.varsity.co.uk/opinion/19419 (last accessed 18 January 2023); Sadiq Khan, 'More BAME people are dying from coronavirus. We have to know why', *Guardian* (19 April 2020). Available at https://www.theguardian.com/commentisfree/2020/apr/19/bame-dying-coronavirus-sadiq-khan (last accessed 18 January 2023).

10 Diane Abbott, 'The disproportionate death of BAME people from #Covid19 and in police custody proves institutional racism is not just an issue for America #BlackLivesMatter' [Twitter post] (8 June 2020). Available at https://twitter.com/HackneyAbbott/status/1270046081804636161 (last accessed 24 February 2023).

11 Dawn Butler, 'Now is the time to get the Government's knee off the neck of the Black, African Caribbean, Asian and minority ethnic community. #BLMUK #COVID19 #BlackLivesMatter' [Twitter post] (18 Jun 2020). Available at https://twitter.com/dawnbutlerbrent/status/1273612140499406850 (last accessed 24 February 2023).

12 Robert Booth, 'Black Lives Matter has increased racial tension, 55% say in UK poll', *Guardian* (27 November 2020). Available at https://www.theguardian.com/world/2020/nov/27/black-lives-matter-has-increased-racial-tension-55-say-in-uk-poll (last accessed 16 January 2023).

13 Matthew Smith, 'Race relations: how have things changed since the 2020 Black Lives Matter protests', YouGov [website] (25 May 2021). Available at https://yougov.co.uk/topics/politics/articles-reports/2021/05/25/race-relations-how-have-things-changed-2020-black- (last accessed 16 January 2023).

14 Rakib Ehsan, 'BLM: a voice for black Britons?' [PDF], Henry Jackson Society [website] (24 February 2021). Available at https://henryjacksonsociety.org/wp-content/uploads/2021/02/BLM-A-Voice-for-Black-Britons-00000002.pdf (last accessed 16 January 2023).

15 Ibid.

16 Ibid.

17 Ibid.

18 Ibid.

19 Nikita Malik and Rakib Ehsan, 'National resilience index 2020: an assessment of the D-10' [PDF], Henry Jackson Society [website] (7 September 2020). Available at https://henryjacksonsociety.org/wp-content/uploads/2020/09/National-Resilience-Index.pdf (last accessed 16 January 2023).

20 Commission on the Future of Multi-Ethnic Britain, *The Future of Multi-Ethnic Britain: The Parekh Report* (London: Profile, 2000).

21 Martin Bentham, 'Critics of a "racist" Britain are misguided, says report', *Telegraph* (8 October 2000). Available at https://www.telegraph.co.uk/news/uknews/1369392/Critics-of-a-racist-Britain-are-misguided-says-report.html (last accessed 16 January 2023).

22 'Anti-discrimination', MIPEX [website]. Available at https://www.mipex.eu/anti-discrimination (last accessed 24 February 2023).

23 European Union Agency for Fundamental Rights, 'Being black in the EU: second European Union minorities and discrimination survey' [PDF] (23 November 2018). Available at https://fra.europa.eu/sites/default/files/fra_uploads/fra-2018-being-black-in-the-eu_en.pdf (last accessed 16 January 2023).

24 Inigo Alexander, 'Now 90% of England agrees: being English is not about colour', *Observer* (30 June 2019). Available at https://www.theguardian.com/society/2019/jun/30/being-english-not-about-colour-say-majority (last accessed 16 January 2023).

25 Runnymede Trust, 'England civil society submission to the United Nations Committee on the Elimination of Racial Discrimination'

[PDF] (July 2021). Available at https://assets.website-files.com/6148 8f992b58e687f1108c7c/61bca661b8abd33d2f6f579c_Runnymede%20 CERD%20report%20v3.pdf (last accessed 16 January 2023).

26 Haroon Siddique, 'UK government accused of pursuing "white nationalist" agenda', *Guardian* (29 December 2020). Available at https://www.theguardian.com/politics/2020/dec/29/uk-government-accused-pursuing-white-nationalist-agenda-runnymede-trust (last accessed 16 January 2023).

1. Why the Left Should Drop 'White Privilege' Theories

1 White House, '"Our priority will be Black, Latino, Asian, and Native American owned small businesses, women-owned businesses, and finally having equal access to resources needed to reopen and rebuild." – President-elect Biden' [Twitter post] (10 January 2021). Available at https://twitter.com/WhiteHouse/status/1348403213 200990209?s=20&t=8PPjYdCglkmsp7IUs7ckbQ (last accessed 24 February 2023).

2 Kamala Harris, 'There's a big difference between equality and equity' [Twitter post] (1 November 2020). Available at https://twitter.com/ KamalaHarris/status/1322963321994289154?s=20&t=8PPjYdCglk msp7IUs7ckbQ (last accessed 24 February 2023).

3 'Republican Glenn Youngkin speech after VA governor win transcript', Rev [website] (2 November 2021). Available at https:// www.rev.com/blog/transcripts/republican-glenn-youngkin-speech-after-va-governor-win-transcript (last accessed 18 January 2023).

4 Quoted in 'A dream of equality of opportunity', UNAC/ UHCP [website]. Available at https://unacuhcp.org/a-dream-of-equality-of-opportunity/#:~:text=%E2%80%9CA%20 dream%20of%20equality%20of,give%20luxuries%20to%20the%20 few.%E2%80%9D&text=Civil%20rights%20leader%20Martin%20 Luther,I%20Have%20a%20Dream%20speech (last accessed 18 January 2023).

5 'Chapter 31: the poor people's campaign' [from *The Autobiography of Martin Luther King, Jr.*, ed. Clayborne Carson (1998)], Martin Luther King, Jr. Research and Education Institute (Stanford University) [website]. Available at https://kinginstitute.stanford.edu/king-papers/

publications/autobiography-martin-luther-king-jr-contents/chapter-31-poor-peoples (last accessed 18 January 2023).

6 Social Mobility Commission, 'Social mobility barometer: public attitudes to social mobility in the UK, 2019 to 2020', Gov.uk [website] (21 January 2020). Available at https://www.gov.uk/government/publications/social-mobility-barometer-poll-results-2019/social-mobility-barometer-public-attitudes-to-social-mobility-in-the-uk-2019-to-2020 (last accessed 16 January 2023).

7 Ibid.

8 'Three in ten workers would run out of money in under a month if they weren't getting paid', Yorkshire Building Society [website] (2021). Available at https://www.ybs.co.uk/w/media-centre/workers-savings (last accessed 18 January 2023).

9 'Average hourly pay', Gov.uk [website] (27 July 2022). Available at https://www.ethnicity-facts-figures.service.gov.uk/work-pay-and-benefits/pay-and-income/average-hourly-pay/latest#by-ethnicity-over-time (last accessed 18 January 2023).

10 'GCSE results (Attainment 8)', Gov.uk [website] (18 March 2022). Available at https://www.ethnicity-facts-figures.service.gov.uk/education-skills-and-training/11-to-16-years-old/gcse-results-attainment-8-for-children-aged-14-to-16-key-stage-4/latest#by-ethnicity (last accessed 18 January 2023).

11 Anita Singh, 'June Sarpong on white privilege: "unfairness is baked into our system"', *Telegraph* (25 December 2020). Available at https://www.telegraph.co.uk/news/2020/12/25/june-sarpong-white-privilege-unfairness-baked-system/ (last accessed 16 January 2023).

12 Sinai Fleary, 'Senior NHS staff told to study "white privilege" in new anti-racism advice on NHS blog', Voice Online [website] (6 September 2021). Available at https://www.voice-online.co.uk/news/2021/09/06/senior-nhs-staff-told-to-study-white-privilege-in-new-anti-racism-advice-on-nhs-blog/ (last accessed 18 January 2023).

13 Ewan Somerville, 'Black Lives Matter training among new diversity courses offered to NHS staff', *Telegraph* (19 September 2021). Available at https://www.telegraph.co.uk/news/2021/09/19/black-lives-matter-training-among-new-diversity-courses-offered/ (last accessed 18 January 2023).

14 Steven Swinford, 'Sajid Javid briefed Tory MPs this afternoon on National Insurance rise for health and social care / He said he will be "watchful for any waste or wokery" from NHS / But it's not clear what concrete commitments from NHS are in exchange for the £16billion of additional funding are' [Twitter post] (8 September 2021). Available at https://twitter.com/steven_swinford/status/1435633122398375940 (last accessed 24 February 2023).

15 'Ethnic differences in life expectancy and mortality from selected causes in England and Wales: 2011 to 2014', Office for National Statistics [website] (26 July 2021). Available at https://www.ons.gov.uk/peoplepopulationandcommunity/birthsdeathsandmarriages/lifeexpectancies/articles/ethnicdifferencesinlifeexpectancyandmortalityfromselectedcausesinenglandandwales/2011to2014#ethnic-breakdown (last accessed 18 January 2023).

16 'Self harm and suicidal thoughts and attempts', Gov.uk [website] (10 October 2017). Available at https://www.ethnicity-facts-figures.service.gov.uk/health/mental-health/adults-reporting-suicidal-thoughts-attempts-and-self-harm/latest#by-ethnicity (last accessed 18 January 2023).

17 Jody Doherty-Cove, 'Brighton council says it is not teaching white privilege to school children', *Argus* (29 June 2021). Available at https://www.theargus.co.uk/news/19405673.brighton-council-says-not-teaching-white-privilege-school-children/ (last accessed 16 January 2023).

18 'Brighton & Hove anti-racist education strategy' [PDF], Brighton & Hove City Council [website]. (March 2022). Available at https://democracy.brighton-hove.gov.uk/documents/s175706/Appendix%201%20-%20Brighton%20and%20Hove%20Anti-Racist%20Education%20Strategy.pdf (last accessed 16 January 2023).

19 Tony Sewell et al., 'Commission on Race and Ethnic Disparities: the report' [PDF], Gov.uk [website] (March 2021). Available at https://assets.publishing.service.gov.uk/government/uploads/system/uploads/attachment_data/file/974507/20210331_-_CRED_Report_-_FINAL_-_Web_Accessible.pdf (last accessed 16 January 2023).

20 Centre for Social Justice, 'Fractured families: why stability matters' [PDF] (June 2013). Available at https://www.centreforsocialjustice.org.uk/wp-content/uploads/2018/02/CSJ_Fractured_Families_Report_WEB_13.06.13-1.pdf (last accessed 16 January 2023).

21 Hope Not Hate, 'Minority communities in the time of COVID & protest: a study of BAME opinion' [PDF] (August 2020). Available

at https://hopenothate.org.uk/wp-content/uploads/2020/08/BAME-report-2020-08-v3-00000003.pdf (last accessed 16 January 2023).

22 'Proportion of children in lone-parent families by ethnic group, England and Wales, 2019', Office for National Statistics [website] (28 June 2021). Available at https://www.ons.gov.uk/peoplepopulationandcommunity/birthsdeathsandmarriages/families/adhocs/12947proportionofchildreninloneparentfamiliesbyethnicgroupenglandandwales2019 (last accessed 16 January 2023).

23 Andrew Sparrow, 'More than half of UK's black children live in poverty, analysis shows', *Guardian* (2 January 2022). Available at https://www.theguardian.com/world/2022/jan/02/more-than-half-of-uks-black-children-live-in-poverty-analysis-shows (last accessed 16 January 2023).

24 Ibid.

25 Quoted ibid.

26 Quoted ibid.

27 Richard Partington, 'Half of all children in lone-parent families are in relative poverty', *Guardian* (4 July 2022). Available at https://www.theguardian.com/business/2022/jul/04/half-of-all-children-in-lone-parent-families-are-in-relative-poverty (last accessed 23 January 2023).

28 'UK poverty 2022: the essential guide to understanding poverty in the UK', Joseph Rowntree Foundation [website] (18 January 2022). Available at https://www.jrf.org.uk/report/uk-poverty-2022 (last accessed 16 January 2023).

29 Mark Dobson, 'Azeem Rafiq apologises for antisemitic messages sent to another player in 2011', *Guardian* (18 November 2021). https://www.theguardian.com/sport/2021/nov/18/azeem-rafiq-apologises-antisemitic-messages-2011-cricket (last accessed 16 January 2023).

30 'Matt Floyd investigates why there is a lack of South Asian players in English cricket', Sky Sports [website] (3 June 2018). Available at https://www.skysports.com/cricket/news/12123/11392595/matt-floyd-investigates-why-there-is-a-lack-of-south-asian-players-in-english-cricket (last accessed 18 January 2023).

31 Quoted in David Coverdale, 'Ajmal Shahzad is one of just a few British Asian coaches in the county game, but Derbyshire's new bowling guru insists: "I've NEVER experienced racism in cricket"', *Daily Mail* (4 April 2021). Available at https://www.dailymail.co.uk/

sport/cricket/article-9435133/Ajmal-Shahzad-discusses-racism-cricket-new-life-Derbyshires-bowling-coach.html (last accessed 27 February 2023).

32 Quoted in Rakib Ehsan, 'When it comes to racism in cricket, we should listen to Shahzad as well as Rafiq', CapX [website] (22 November 2021). Available at https://capx.co/when-it-comes-to-racism-in-cricket-we-should-listen-to-ajmal-shahzad-as-well-as-azeem-rafiq/ (last accessed 27 February 2023).

33 'New CSI report on ethnic minority job discrimination', Nuffield College, University of Oxford [website] (21 January 19). Available at https://www.nuffield.ox.ac.uk/news-events/news/new-csi-report-on-ethnic-minority-job-discrimination/ (last accessed 24 February 2023).

34 Rakib Ehsan, 'Discrimination, social relations and trust: civic inclusion of British ethnic minorities' [PhD thesis, Egham, Royal Holloway, University of London, 2019]. Available at https://pure.royalholloway.ac.uk/en/publications/discrimination-social-relations-and-trust-civic-inclusion-of-brit (last accessed 18 January 2023).

35 Robert Booth, 'Secret Pontins blacklist prevented people with Irish surnames from booking', *Guardian* (2 March 2021). Available at https://www.theguardian.com/uk-news/2021/mar/02/secret-pontins-blacklist-irish-surnames (last accessed 18 January 2023).

2. Labour's Identity-Politics Problem

1 Jeremy Corbyn, 'Only Labour can be trusted to unlock the talent of Black, Asian and Minority Ethnic people' [Twitter post] (30 May 2017). Available at https://twitter.com/jeremycorbyn/status/869571607060070401?s=20&t=o4U65T1at3pPttjDNLG9Fw (last accessed 24 February 2023).

2 'Aaron Bastani: "What I really said about the poppy"' [video], YouTube (14 November 2018). Available at https://www.youtube.com/watch?v=pv1_p8PE5vg (last accessed 24 February 2023).

3 Labour Party, 'Labour party race & faith manifesto' [PDF] (2019). Available at https://labour.org.uk/wp-content/uploads/2019/11/Race-and-Faith-Manifesto-2019.pdf (last accessed 19 January 2023).

4 All-Party Parliamentary Group on British Muslims, 'Islamophobia defined: the inquiry into a working definition of

Islamophobia' (2018). Available at https://static1.squarespace.com/static/599c3d2febbd1a90cffdd8a9/t/5bfd1ea3352f531a6170ce ee/1543315109493/Islamophobia+Defined.pdf (last accessed 16 January 2023).

5 Ibid.

6 Rakib Ehsan, 'Muslim anti-Semitism in contemporary Great Britain' [PDF], Henry Jackson Society [website] (March 2020). Available at https://henryjacksonsociety.org/wp-content/uploads/2020/08/HJS-British-Muslim-Anti-Semitism-Report-web-1.pdf (last accessed 16 January 2023).

7 Nimco Ali, 'I sense this definition of #Islamophobia is going to mean that a lot of us feminist and secular Muslim women will be called Islamophobic for seeking to uphold the basic human rights and freedoms of women and for questing [*sic*] male interpretation of holy text' [Twitter post] (15 May 2019). Available at https://twitter.com/NimkoAli/status/1128580382402785280 (last accessed 24 February 2023).

8 'Who we are', Islamic Human Rights Commission (IHRC) [website]. Available at https://www.ihrc.org.uk/about-us/ (last accessed 24 February 2023).

9 'Our aims & objectives', Islamic Human Rights Commission (IHRC) [website]. Available at https://www.ihrc.org.uk/aims-and-objectives/ (last accessed 24 February 2023).

10 Laura O'Callaghan, 'Pro-Iranian group chief "praised fatwa against Salman Rushdie"', National UK [website] (21 August 2022). Available at https://www.thenationalnews.com/world/uk-news/2022/08/21/uk-islamic-group-chief-praised-fatwa-against-salman-rushdie/ (last accessed 18 January 2023).

11 Max Aitchison, 'Chairman of a British-based Islamic Human Rights Commission – that has has [*sic*] received more than £1.4 million in charity cash – praised the fatwa on Sir Salman Rushdie less than a year ago', *Mail on Sunday* (21 August 2022). Available at https://www.dailymail.co.uk/news/article-11130693/Chairman-British-based-Islamic-Human-Rights-Commission-praised-fatwa-Sir-Salman-Rushdie.html (last accessed 19 January 2023).

12 Quoted in Robert Mendick, 'Outrage as Islamist claims Grenfell Tower victims were "murdered by Zionists" who fund Conservative Party', *Telegraph* (8 July 2017). Available at https://www.telegraph.

co.uk/news/2017/07/08/outrage-islamist-claims-grenfell-tower-victims-murdered-zionists/ (last accessed 19 January 2023).

13 Paul Stott, 'Iranian influence networks in the United Kingdom: audit and analysis' [PDF], Henry Jackson Society [website] (2021). Available at https://henryjacksonsociety.org/wp-content/uploads/2021/06/HJS-Iranian-Influence-Networks-in-the-UK-Report-HR-web-1.pdf (last accessed 18 January 2023).

14 Quoted in Andrew Norfolk, 'Iran "propaganda" group IHRC gets £1.2m from taxpayer-backed charity', *Times* (10 October 2019). Available at https://www.thetimes.co.uk/article/iran-propaganda-group-ihrc-gets-1-2m-from-taxpayer-backed-charity-r2lh7jkc9 (last accessed 16 January 2023).

15 Emma Fox, 'Islamic Human Rights Commission: advocating for the Ayatollahs' [PDF], Henry Jackson Society [website]. Available at https://henryjacksonsociety.org/shop-hjs/islamic-human-rights-commission-advocating-for-the-ayatollahs/ (last accessed 22 February 2023).

16 Lee Harpin, 'Nearly 40 per cent of Jews would "seriously consider" emigrating if Corbyn became PM', *Jewish Chronicle* (5 September 2018). Available at https://www.thejc.com/news/uk-news/nearly-40-per-cent-of-british-jews-would-seriously-consider-emigrating-if-corbyn-became-pm-1.469270 (last accessed 16 January 2023).

17 'David Lammy and Andrew Neil on tower block death claims', BBC News [website] (20 July 2017). Available at https://www.bbc.co.uk/news/av/uk-politics-40672349 (last accessed 19 January 2023).

18 Laura Hughes, 'Grenfell row as Labour MP suggests "white, upper-middle class man" should not have been hired to lead inquiry', *Telegraph* (2 July 2017). Available at https://www.telegraph.co.uk/news/2017/07/02/labour-mp-suggests-white-upper-middle-class-grenfell-judge-has/ (last accessed 19 January 2023).

19 Adam Forrest, 'Labour's David Lammy questions why "Black English" is not an option on census', *Independent* (3 August 2021). Available at https://www.independent.co.uk/news/uk/politics/david-lammy-black-english-census-b1895736.html (last accessed 28 February 2023).

20 Clive Lewis, 'Move along. Nothing to see here. #RaceReport' [Twitter post] (31 March 2021). Available at https://twitter.com/labourlewis/status/1377344415681814528?s=20&t=yMr6-oBr_5286pm2sPOIxA

(last accessed 24 February 2023). For the report, see Tony Sewell et al., 'Commission on Race and Ethnic Disparities: the report' [PDF], Gov.uk [website] (March 2021). Available at https://assets.publishing. service.gov.uk/government/uploads/system/uploads/attachment_ data/file/974507/20210331_-_CRED_Report_-_FINAL_-_Web_ Accessible.pdf (last accessed 16 January 2023).

21 Jessica Elgot, 'Labour defends new strategy to focus on patriotism and union flag', *Guardian* (3 February 2021). Available at https:// www.theguardian.com/politics/2021/feb/03/labour-defends-new-strategy-to-focus-on-patriotism-and-union-flag (last accessed 19 January 2023).

22 Quoted in Aditya Chakrabortty and Jessica Elgot, 'Leak reveals Labour plan to focus on flag and patriotism to win back voters', *Guardian* (2 February 2021). Available at https://www.theguardian. com/politics/2021/feb/02/labour-urged-to-focus-on-flag-and-patriotism-to-win-voters-trust-leak-reveals (last accessed 19 January 2023).

23 'Watch: Badenoch calls Dawn Butler's hate-stoking race comments "disgraceful"', Guido Fawkes [website] (20 April 2021). Available at https://order-order.com/2021/04/20/watch-badenoch-calls-dawn-butlers-hate-stoking-race-comments-disgraceful/ (last accessed 19 January 2023).

24 Dr Shola Mos-Shogbamimu, 'Racist Boris Johnson "Race Commission" fronted by token Black man, Tony Sewell, finds Institutional Racism doesn't exist / A #WhiteSupremacy LIE to gaslight entire nation #ThisIsWhyIResist / Britain. Is. Not. A. Model. Of. Racial. Equality.#BlackLivesMatter' [Twitter post] (31 March 2021). Available at https://twitter.com/SholaMos1/status/13771563 95842248704?s=20&t=6UUVFMTEDuQBLW5qHTXNUw (last accessed 24 February 2023).

25 Kehinde Andrews, 'Trevor "formerly of the Black community" Phillips should have lost all support from Black folk long ago. I wrote this piece for @OBU_BlackUnity a while back when #TrevorPhillips was indulging in what Malcolm would have called "modern day Uncle Tom coonery"' [Twitter post] (9 March 2020). Available at https://twitter.com/kehinde_andrews/status/123700799279461581 0?s=20&t=4RRgyX5TaKvmBhIiPX4rkw (last accessed 24 February 2023).

26 Quoted in Dave Clark, 'MP Claudia Webbe to be sentenced for harassment campaign that included acid attack threat', ChronicleLive [website] (4 November 2021). Available at https://www.chroniclelive.co.uk/news/uk-news/mp-claudia-webbe-sentenced-harassment-22062449 (last accessed 20 January 2023).

27 Quoted in 'Leicester East Labour chairman quits "laughing stock" party', BBC News [website] (18 November 2019). Available at https://www.bbc.co.uk/news/election-2019-50467321 (last accessed 20 January 2023).

28 Naomi Canton, 'PIO Labour activist quits, says Labour is overrun with Marxists and party is institutionally "anti-Indian"', *Times of India* (1 September 2020). Available at https://timesofindia.indiatimes.com/world/uk/pio-labour-activist-quits-says-labour-is-overrun-with-marxists-and-party-is-institutionally-anti-indian/articleshow/77878090.cms?utm_source=twitter.com&utm_medium=social&utm_campaign=TOIDesktop (last accessed 20 January 2023).

29 Dan Martin, 'Leicester East MP Claudia Webbe breached code of conduct over Islington councillor payments', LeicestershireLive [website] (15 February 2021). Available at https://www.leicestermercury.co.uk/news/leicester-news/leicester-east-mp-claudia-webbe-5004445 (last accessed 20 January 2023).

30 Naz Shah, 'Prevent has failed and it has alienated the Muslim community #BradfordWest' [Twitter post] (31 May 2017). Available at https://twitter.com/NazShahBfd/status/869987006373384193?s=20&t=6UUVFMTEDuQBLW5qHTXNUw (last accessed 24 February 2023).

31 Jon Clements, Manon Roberts and Dan Forman, 'Listening to British Muslims: policing, extremism and Prevent' [PDF] (March 2020). Available at https://b9cf6cd4-6aad-4419-a368-724e7d1352b9.usrfiles.com/ugd/b9cf6c_d12a4911772d4e04a683b69561c86501.pdf (last accessed 16 January 2023).

3. In Defence of the Family

1 'Proportion of children in lone-parent families by ethnic group, England and Wales, 2019', Office for National Statistics [website] (28 June 2021). Available at https://www.ons.gov.uk/peoplepopulationandcommunity/birthsdeathsandmarriages/families/adhocs/12947proportionofchildreninloneparentfamiliesbyethnicgroupenglandandwales2019 (last accessed 16 January 2023).

2   Ibid.

3   Ibid.

4   Ibid.

5   Rachel de Souza, 'Family and its protective effect: part 1 of the Independent Family Review' [PDF], Children's Commissioner [website] (September 2022). Available at https://www.childrenscommissioner.gov.uk/wp-content/uploads/2022/12/cc-family-and-its-protective-effect-part-1-of-the-independent-family-review-.pdf (last accessed 16 January 2023).

6   Sarah Harris, 'REVEALED – the scale of family breakdown in modern Britain laid bare: half of children live across more than one household and a quarter of families are headed by a lone parent (and 90 PER CENT are women), shocking new figures show', *Daily Mail* (1 September 2022). Available at https://www.dailymail.co.uk/news/article-11166817/Family-breakdown-modern-Britain-laid-bare-Half-children-live-one-household.html (last accessed 20 January 2023).

7   Sophia Worringer, 'Marriage still matters – and most for the poorest', ConservativeHome [website] (16 August 2020). Available at https://conservativehome.com/2020/08/16/sophia-worringer-marriage-still-matters-and-most-for-the-poorest/ (last accessed 16 January 2023).

8   Rob Henderson, 'Does poverty create psychopathic behavior? No, but family instability appears to', Institute for Family Studies [website] (13 July 2021). Available at https://ifstudies.org/blog/does-poverty-create-psychopathic-behavior-no-but-family-instability-appears-to (last accessed 22 January 2023).

9   Tony Sewell et al., 'Commission on Race and Ethnic Disparities: the report' [PDF], Gov.uk [website] (March 2021). Available at https://assets.publishing.service.gov.uk/government/uploads/system/uploads/attachment_data/file/974507/20210331_-_CRED_Report_-_FINAL_-_Web_Accessible.pdf (last accessed 16 January 2023).

10   Carlijn Bussemakers, Gerbert Kraaykamp and Jochem Tolsma, 'Variation in the educational consequences of parental death and

divorce: the role of family and country characteristics' [PDF], *Demographic Research* 46/20 (31 March 2022), 581–618. Available at https://www.demographic-research.org/volumes/vol46/20/46-20.pdf (last accessed 16 January 2023).

11 Sophia Worringer, 'Family structure still matters' [PDF], Centre for Social Justice [website] (August 2020). Available at https://www.centreforsocialjustice.org.uk/wp-content/uploads/2020/10/CSJJ8372-Family-structure-Report-200807.pdf (last accessed 16 January 2023).

12 'Families and households in the UK: 2021', Office for National Statistics [website] (9 March 2022). Available at https://www.ons.gov.uk/peoplepopulationandcommunity/birthsdeathsandmarriages/families/bulletins/familiesandhouseholds/2021#:~:text=In%202021%2C%20there%20were%203.0,the%20North%20East%20of%20England (last accessed 20 January 2023).

13 'Marriages in England and Wales: 2019', Office for National Statistics [website] (19 May 2022). Available at https://www.ons.gov.uk/peoplepopulationandcommunity/birthsdeathsandmarriages/marriagecohabitationandcivilpartnerships/bulletins/marriagesinenglandandwalesprovisional/2019 (last accessed 20 January 2023).

14 Ibid.

15 Worringer, 'Family structure still matters'.

16 C. S. Henry, 'Family system characteristics, parental behaviors, and adolescent family life satisfaction', *Family Relations: An Interdisciplinary Journal of Applied Family Studies* 43/4 (1994), 447–55.

17 ICM Unlimited, 'Exploring the topic of race, identity and community relations among Black British people', Walnut Social Research [website] (2021). Available at https://www.icmunlimited.com/our-work/exploring-the-topic-of-race-identity-and-community-relations-among-black-british-people/ (last accessed 18 January 2023).

18 Ibid.

19 Ibid.

20 Rakib Ehsan, 'BLM: a voice for black Britons?' [PDF], Henry Jackson Society [website] (24 February 2021). Available at https://henryjacksonsociety.org/wp-content/uploads/2021/02/BLM-A-Voice-for-Black-Britons-00000002.pdf (last accessed 16 January 2023).

21 Sewell et al., 'Commission on Race and Ethnic Disparities: the report'.

22 Shulamith Firestone, *The Dialectic of Sex: The Case for Feminist Revolution* (New York: William Morrow, 1970).

23 Cristina Odone, 'Family, far more than school, shapes children's outcomes. Britain's next PM must understand that, writes Cristina Odone', *Daily Mail* (1 September 2022). Available at https://www.dailymail.co.uk/debate/article-11167067/Family-far-school-shapes-childrens-outcomes-writes-CRISTINA-ODONE.html (last accessed 24 February 2023).

4. The Power of Faith

1 Institute for Economics & Peace, 'Global terrorism index 2022: measuring the impact of terrorism' [PDF] (March 2022). Available at https://www.visionofhumanity.org/wp-content/uploads/2022/03/GTI-2022-web-04112022.pdf (last accessed 16 December 2022).

2 Rakib Ehsan, 'BLM: a voice for black Britons?' [PDF], Henry Jackson Society [website] (24 February 2021). Available at https://henryjacksonsociety.org/wp-content/uploads/2021/02/BLM-A-Voice-for-Black-Britons-00000002.pdf (last accessed 16 January 2023).

3 ICM Unlimited, 'Exploring the topic of race, identity and community relations among Black British people', Walnut Social Research [website] (2021). Available at https://www.icmunlimited.com/our-work/exploring-the-topic-of-race-identity-and-community-relations-among-black-british-people/ (last accessed 18 January 2023).

4 Rakib Ehsan, 'Muslim anti-Semitism in contemporary Great Britain' [PDF], Henry Jackson Society [website] (March 2020). Available at https://henryjacksonsociety.org/wp-content/uploads/2020/08/HJS-British-Muslim-Anti-Semitism-Report-web-1.pdf (last accessed 16 January 2023).

5 ICM Unlimited, 'Exploring the topic of race, identity and community relations among Black British people'.

6 Ibid.

7 P. S. Mueller, D. J. Plevak and T. A. Rummans, 'Religious involvement, spirituality, and medicine: implications for clinical practice', *Mayo Clinic Proceedings* 76/12 (2001), 1225–35.

8 Robin Dunbar, 'The big idea: do we still need religion?', *Guardian* (28 March 2022). Available at https://www.theguardian.com/books/2022/mar/28/the-big-idea-do-we-still-need-religion (last accessed 16 January 2023).

9 Markus Jokela, 'Religiosity, psychological distress, and well-being: evaluating familial confounding with multicohort sibling data', *American Journal of Epidemiology* 191/4 (2021), 584–90.

10 W. Bradford Wilcox and Nicholas H. Wolfinger, *Soul Mates: Religion, Sex, Love, and Marriage among African Americans and Latinos* (New York: Oxford University Press, 2016).

11 Ehsan, 'BLM: a voice for black Britons?'

12 Tomiwa Owolade, 'The future of Anglicanism is African', UnHerd [website] (15 April (2022). Available at https://unherd.com/2022/04/the-future-of-anglicanism-is-african/ (last accessed 20 January 2023).

13 Nicole Martin and Omar Khan, 'Ethnic minorities at the 2017 general election' [PDF], Runnymede Trust [website] (February 2019). Available at https://assets.website-files.com/61488f992b58e687f1108c7c/61c3125671c8d5a0ce3c59c5_2017%20Election%20Briefing%20(1).pdf (last accessed 16 January 2023).

14 'Ethnic group, England and Wales: census 2021', Office for National Statistics [website] (29 November 2022). Available at https://www.ons.gov.uk/peoplepopulationandcommunity/culturalidentity/ethnicity/bulletins/ethnicgroupenglandandwales/census2021 (last accessed 20 January 2023).

15 Swaran Singh, 'The Singh investigation: independent investigation into alleged discrimination: citing protected characteristics within the Conservative and Unionist Party in England, Wales and Northern Ireland' [PDF] (21 May 2021). Available at https://singhinvestigation.co.uk/wp-content/uploads/2021/06/Singh_Investigation_Report_for_download.pdf (last accessed 16 January 2023).

16 Ehsan, 'Muslim anti-Semitism in contemporary Great Britain'.

5. Britain's Ethnic-Minority Patriots

1 Matthew Prior, 'UK prejudice against immigrants amongst lowest in Europe', Frontiers Science News [website] (26 February 2019). Available at https://blog.frontiersin.org/2019/02/26/uk-prejudice-

against-immigrants-amongst-lowest-in-europe/ (last accessed 16 January 2023). The original article is M. D. R. Evans and Jonathan Kelley, 'Prejudice against immigrants symptomizes a larger syndrome, is strongly diminished by socioeconomic development, and the UK is not an outlier: insights from the WVS, EVS, and EQLS surveys', *Frontiers in Sociology* 4/12 (2019). Available at https://www.frontiersin.org/articles/10.3389/fsoc.2019.00012/full?utm_source=fweb&utm_medium=nblog&utm_campaign=ba-sci-fsoc-prejudice-immigrants (last accessed 6 March 2023).

2   Aditya Chakrabortty, 'Keir Starmer's patriot act risks turning off his core Labour voters', *Guardian* (2 February 2021). Available at https://www.theguardian.com/politics/2021/feb/02/keir-starmer-patriot-act-risks-turning-off-core-labour-voters (last accessed 18 January 2023).

3   Taj Ali, 'Labour is in danger of alienating ethnic minority voters by appealing to nationalists', *Independent* (23 September 2020). Available at https://www.independent.co.uk/voices/labour-ethnic-minority-nationalist-right-wing-voters-election-b551496.html (last accessed 18 January 2023).

4   Nesrine Malik, 'Keir Starmer's "new management" will cost Labour minority votes. Does he care?', *Guardian* (27 September 2020). Available at https://www.theguardian.com/commentisfree/2020/sep/27/keir-starmer-labour-minority-votes-red-wall-tory (last accessed 18 January 2023).

5   ICM Unlimited, 'Exploring the topic of race, identity and community relations among Black British people', Walnut Social Research [website] (2021). Available at https://www.icmunlimited.com/our-work/exploring-the-topic-of-race-identity-and-community-relations-among-black-british-people/ (last accessed 18 January 2023).

6   Ibid.

7   Ibid.

8   Inigo Alexander, 'Now 90% of England agrees: being English is not about colour', *Observer* (30 June 2019). Available at https://www.theguardian.com/society/2019/jun/30/being-english-not-about-colour-say-majority (last accessed 16 January 2023).

9   Ibid.

10   Sunder Katwala, John Denham and Steve Ballinger, 'Beyond a 90-minute nation: why it's time for an inclusive England outside the stadium' [PDF], British Future [website] (2021). Available at https://

www.britishfuture.org/wp-content/uploads/2021/06/Beyond-a-90-minute-nation.-Inclusive-England-report.10.6.21.pdf (last accessed 18 January 2023).

11 European Union Agency for Fundamental Rights, 'Being black in the EU: second European Union minorities and discrimination survey' [PDF] (23 November 2018). Available at https://fra.europa.eu/sites/default/files/fra_uploads/fra-2018-being-black-in-the-eu_en.pdf (last accessed 16 January 2023).

12 Ibid.

13 Quoted in Alexander, 'Now 90% of England agrees: being English is not about colour'.

14 Paul Mason, 'I do not want to be English – and any attempt to create an English identity will fail', *Guardian* (10 May 2015). Available at https://www.theguardian.com/commentisfree/2015/may/10/snp-english-national-identity-class-cultural-divide (last accessed 18 January 2023).

6. Britain's Ethnic Minorities and their Democracy

1 Commission on the Future of Multi-Ethnic Britain, *The Future of Multi-Ethnic Britain: The Parekh Report* (London: Profile, 2000).

2 Tony Sewell et al., 'Commission on Race and Ethnic Disparities: the report' [PDF], Gov.uk [website] (March 2021). Available at https://assets.publishing.service.gov.uk/government/uploads/system/uploads/attachment_data/file/974507/20210331_-_CRED_Report_-_FINAL_-_Web_Accessible.pdf (last accessed 16 January 2023).

3 Nikita Malik and Rakib Ehsan, 'National resilience index 2020: an assessment of the D-10' [PDF], Henry Jackson Society [website] (7 September 2020). Available at https://henryjacksonsociety.org/wp-content/uploads/2020/09/National-Resilience-Index.pdf (last accessed 16 January 2023).

4 Anthony F. Heath, Stephen D. Fisher, Gemma Rosenblatt, David Sanders and Maria Sobolewska, *The Political Integration of Ethnic Minorities in Britain* (Oxford: Oxford University Press, 2013).

5 Rakib Ehsan, 'Discrimination, social relations and trust: civic inclusion of British ethnic minorities' [PhD thesis, Egham, Royal Holloway, University of London, 2019]. Available at https://pure.

royalholloway.ac.uk/en/publications/discrimination-social-relations-and-trust-civic-inclusion-of-brit (last accessed 18 January 2023).

6 Ibid.

7 Ibid.

8 Ibid.

9 Ibid.

10 Ibid.

11 Jon Clements, Manon Roberts and Dan Forman, 'Listening to British Muslims: policing, extremism and Prevent' [PDF] (March 2020). Available at https://b9cf6cd4-6aad-4419-a368-724e7d1352b9. usrfiles.com/ugd/b9cf6c_d12a4911772d4e04a683b69561c86501.pdf (last accessed 16 January 2023).

12 Ibid.

13 'Confidence in the local police', Gov.uk [website] (12 May 2021). Available at https://www.ethnicity-facts-figures.service.gov.uk/crime-justice-and-the-law/policing/confidence-in-the-local-police/latest#by-ethnicity-over-time (last accessed 18 January 2023).

14 Clements, Roberts and Forman, 'Listening to British Muslims: policing, extremism and Prevent'.

15 Ibid.

16 Quoted in 'EU companies can ban headscarves under certain conditions, court says', Reuters [website] (15 July 2021). Available at https://www.reuters.com/world/europe/top-eu-court-says-headscarves-can-be-banned-work-under-certain-conditions-2021-07-15/ (last accessed 16 January 2023).

17 Rakib Ehsan, 'BLM: a voice for black Britons?' [PDF], Henry Jackson Society [website] (24 February 2021). Available at https://henryjacksonsociety.org/wp-content/uploads/2021/02/BLM-A-Voice-for-Black-Britons-00000002.pdf (last accessed 16 January 2023).

18 Ibid.

19 Ehsan, 'Discrimination, social relations and trust: civic inclusion of British ethnic minorities'.

20 Quoted in Stephen Cook, 'Scarman report into Brixton riots published – archive, 1981', *Guardian* (26 November 2021). Available at https://www.theguardian.com/world/2021/nov/26/scarman-report-into-brixton-riots-published-archive-1981 (last accessed 20 January 2023).

21 Ehsan, 'BLM: a voice for black Britons?'

22 'Baroness Casey Review – final report' [PDF], Metropolitan Police [website] (March 2023). Available at https://www.met.police.uk/police-forces/metropolitan-police/areas/about-us/about-the-met/bcr/baroness-casey-review/ (last accessed 20 April 2023).

23 Nick Ferris, 'How police stop and search remains racially biased', *New Statesman* (28 July 2021). Available at https://www.newstatesman.com/politics/2021/07/how-police-stop-and-search-remains-racially-biased (last accessed 20 January 2023).

24 'Stop and search', Liberty [website]. Available at https://www.libertyhumanrights.org.uk/fundamental/stop-and-search/ (last accessed 24 February 2023).

25 'Crime in England and Wales: year ending March 2020', Office for National Statistics [website] (17 July 2020). Available at https://www.ons.gov.uk/peoplepopulationandcommunity/crimeandjustice/bulletins/crimeinenglandandwales/yearendingmarch2020 (last accessed 20 January 2023).

26 'London's knife crime hotspots revealed', BBC News [website] (7 October 2019). Available at https://www.bbc.co.uk/news/uk-england-london-49921421 (last accessed 20 January 2023).

27 'Understanding ethnic disparities in involvement in crime – a limited scope rapid evidence review, by Professor Clifford Stott et al', Gov.uk [website] (28 April 2021). Available at https://www.gov.uk/government/publications/the-report-of-the-commission-on-race-and-ethnic-disparities-supporting-research/understanding-ethnic-disparities-in-involvement-in-crime-a-limited-scope-rapid-evidence-review-by-professor-clifford-stott-et-al (last accessed 20 January 2023).

28 'Press release: calls for a commission on knife crime in the black community', Mayor of London / London Assembly [website] (10 February 2022). Available at https://www.london.gov.uk/press-releases/assembly/commission-on-knife-crime-in-black-community#:~:text=This%20Assembly%20is%20concerned%20that,53%25%20of%20knife%20crime%20perpetrators (last accessed 20 January 2023).

29 'Confidence in the local police'.

30 Rosie Carter, 'Minority communities in the time of COVID & protest: a study of BAME opinion' [PDF], Hope Not Hate [website]

(August 2020). Available at https://hopenothate.org.uk/wp-content/uploads/2020/08/BAME-report-2020-08-v3-00000003.pdf (last accessed 16 January 2023).

31 Sewell et al., 'Commission on Race and Ethnic Disparities: the report'.

32 Quoted in Tony Diver, 'Outrage as Labour MP says Rishi Sunak as PM "isn't a win for Asian representation"', *Telegraph* (24 October 2022). Available at https://www.telegraph.co.uk/politics/2022/10/24/outrage-labour-mp-says-rishi-sunak-pm-isnt-win-asian-representation/ (last accessed 20 January 2023).

33 Faiza Shaheen, 'To all those getting ready to write a piece celebrating having first poc PM & how this means any poc can do it if they work hard enough. Please remember: / 1. He's very rich & went to top private school / 2. He supports the orthodoxies/ is the establishment / 3. No one voted for him' [Twitter post] (23 October 2022). Available at https://twitter.com/faizashaheen/status/1584293120950546432 (last accessed 24 February 2023).

34 'Rupa Huq MP apologises for "superficially" black remark', BBC News [website] (28 September 2022). Available at https://www.bbc.co.uk/news/uk-politics-63050482 (last accessed 20 January 2023).

35 'Rishi Sunak: I took money from deprived urban areas' [video of Sky News report], YouTube (5 August 2022). Available at https://www.youtube.com/watch?v=xegB9J-mn1A (last accessed 7 February 2023).

36 'Resurfaced clip captures Rishi Sunak suggesting he doesn't have "working class" friends' [video from *The Independent*], YouTube (11 July 2022). Available at https://www.youtube.com/watch?v=p9bbBYcwFOk (last accessed 7 February 2023).

37 Matt Singh, 'Stephen Lawrence: has Britain changed?', Number Cruncher Politics [website] (20 July 2020). Available at https://www.ncpolitics.uk/2020/07/stephen-lawrence-has-britain-changed/ (last accessed 18 January 2023).

7. Ethnic-Minority Academic and Professional Advancement

1 Black Lives Matter UK, 'It's Monday, which means it's as good a time as any to remind you of our key demands (in case you missed them in our last Go Fund Me update). We believe all these things are necessary and possible. #BlackLivesMatter #theukisnotinnocent' [Twitter post] (21 September 2020). Available at https://twitter.com/ ukblm/status/1308065339041869827 (last accessed 24 February 2023).

2 'Ethnicity pay gaps: 2019', Office for National Statistics [website] (12 October 2020). Available at https://www. ons.gov.uk/employmentandlabourmarket/peopleinwork/ earningsandworkinghours/articles/ethnicitypaygapsingreatbritain/2 019#ethnicity-breakdowns (last accessed 20 January 2023).

3 A. B. K. Kasozi, *The Social Origins of Violence In Uganda: 1964–1985* (London: McGill–Queen's University Press, 1994).

4 'Proportion of children in lone-parent families by ethnic group, England and Wales, 2019', Office for National Statistics [website] (28 June 2021). Available at https://www.ons.gov.uk/ peoplepopulationandcommunity/birthsdeathsandmarriages/families/ adhocs/12947proportionofchildreninloneparentfamiliesbyethnicgrou penglandandwales2019 (last accessed 16 January 2023).

5 'GCSE results (Attainment 8)', Gov.uk [website] (18 March 2022). Available at https://www.ethnicity-facts-figures.service.gov. uk/education-skills-and-training/11-to-16-years-old/gcse-results-attainment-8-for-children-aged-14-to-16-key-stage-4/latest#by-ethnicity (last accessed 18 January 2023).

6 'Academic year 2018/19: permanent exclusions and suspensions in England', Gov.uk (30 July 2020). Available at https://explore-education-statistics.service.gov.uk/find-statistics/permanent-and-fixed-period-exclusions-in-england/2018-19 (last accessed 18 January 2023).

7 Samir Shah, 'The success of British Indians is troubling for some. Why?', *Spectator* (20 June 2020). Available at https://www.spectator. co.uk/article/the-success-of-british-indians-is-troubling-for-some-why/ (last accessed 20 January 2023).

8 Quoted ibid.

9 'Religion, England and Wales: Census 2021', Office for National Statistics [website] (29 November 2022). Available at https://www. ons.gov.uk/peoplepopulationandcommunity/culturalidentity/religion/ bulletins/religionenglandandwales/census2021#:~:text=There%20 were%20increases%20in%20the,%2C%201.5%25%20in%202011) (last accessed 20 January 2023).

10 Shah, 'The success of British Indians is troubling for some. Why?'

11 Rishi Sunak, 'A good education is the closest thing we have to a silver bullet when it comes to making people's lives better. / Read my plans to radically reform education to put British kids ahead [...] Join the team Ready4Rishi.com' [Twitter post] (7 August 2022). Available at https://twitter.com/RishiSunak/status/1556205995621326850?s=20&t=Oz4KS5Fq9VrE_gW8yCs1BA (last accessed 24 February 2023).

12 Lucinda Platt and Carolina V. Zuccotti, 'Second-generation ethnic minorities are achieving great success in education, but this does not translate into equal success in the labour market', Institute for Fiscal Studies [website] (29 June 2021). Available at https://ifs.org.uk/news/second-generation-ethnic-minorities-are-achieving-great-success-education-does-not-translate (last accessed 18 January 2023).

13 'GCSE results (Attainment 8)'.

14 Sian Griffiths, 'The motto of Michaela, the school led by @Miss_Snuffy is "Work hard, be kind". Do such mottos encourage black and global majority pupils to be compliant and subservient? Similar school mottos have been "retired" in the US on such grounds @thesundaytimes' [Twitter post] (16 January 2023). Available at https://twitter.com/SianGriffiths6/status/1482640235745976324 (last accessed 24 February 2023).

15 Andrew Sparrow, 'More than half of UK's black children live in poverty, analysis shows', *Guardian* (2 January 2022). Available at https://www.theguardian.com/world/2022/jan/02/more-than-half-of-uks-black-children-live-in-poverty-analysis-shows (last accessed 16 January 2023).

16 Ibid.

17 'GCSE results (Attainment 8)'.

18 Ibid.

19 Ibid.

20 'Academic year 2018/19: permanent exclusions and suspensions in England', Gov.uk (30 July 2020). Available at https://explore-education-statistics.service.gov.uk/find-statistics/permanent-and-fixed-period-exclusions-in-england/2018-19 (last accessed 18 January 2023).

21 'GCSE results (Attainment 8)'.

8. Towards a Relevant Traditional Left

1   Rakib Ehsan, 'BLM: a voice for black Britons?' [PDF], Henry Jackson Society [website] (24 February 2021). Available at https://henryjacksonsociety.org/wp-content/uploads/2021/02/BLM-A-Voice-for-Black-Britons-00000002.pdf (last accessed 16 January 2023).

2   Ibid.

3   'Baroness Casey Review – final report' [PDF], Metropolitan Police [website] (March 2023). Available at https://www.met.police.uk/police-forces/metropolitan-police/areas/about-us/about-the-met/bcr/baroness-casey-review/ (last accessed 20 April 2023).

4   Rakib Ehsan, 'Our society: integrating Britain's communities' [PDF]. Available at https://rakibehsan.com/wp-content/uploads/2023/02/Rakib-Ehsan-Integrating-Britains-Communities-Report-1.pdf (last accessed 24 February 2023).

5   'Diversity wins: how inclusion matters', McKinsey & Company [website] (19 May 2020). Available at https://www.mckinsey.com/featured-insights/diversity-and-inclusion/diversity-wins-how-inclusion-matters (last accessed 2 January 2023).

6   Ruby McGregor-Smith, 'Race in the workplace: the McGregor-Smith review' [PDF], Gov.uk [website] (2017). Available at https://assets.publishing.service.gov.uk/government/uploads/system/uploads/attachment_data/file/594336/race-in-workplace-mcgregor-smith-review.pdf (last accessed 2 January 2023).

7   Quoted in 'The Indian Army in the Second World War', Commonwealth War Graves Commission [website]. Available at https://web.archive.org/web/20120404114825/http://www.cwgc.org/foreverindia/context/indian-army-in-2nd-world-war.php (last accessed 20 April 2023).

8   Quoted in 'For Jews, the queen represented everything that we love about this country', *Jewish Chronicle* (9 September 2022). Available at https://www.thejc.com/lets-talk/all/for-jews-the-queen-represented-everything-that-we-love-about-this-country-5gU3h1j48HTZ9BJy2poB5X#:~:text=Lord%20Finkelstein's%20grandmother%2C%20herself%20a,has%20always%20mattered%20so%20much (last accessed 18 January 2023).